"NAKED INTO

PRIMITIVE
WILDERNESS SKILLS,
APPLIED & ADVANCED

By John & Geri McPherson

"Naked into the Wilderness - 2",
Primitive Wilderness Skills, Applied & Advanced

By John & Geri McPherson

Prairie Wolf
John & Geri McPherson
POB 96, Randolph, KS 66554

ISBN 0-9678777-8-4

Printer: Letromac Design & Printing, Inc.

First printing November 1996
Second printing October 1998
Third printing October 1999
Fourth printing March 2001
Fifth printing September 2002

Printed in Canada

CONTENTS

for

Argel Pultz

*Who sweated with me thru our
first ever bow drill fire,
and who was there at first light,
every day we built our home.*

INTRODUCTION

Me, Geri, friend Ivan and Smoke, somewhere in Idaho.

*T*his is the second large book that we have put together. The first, **"NAKED INTO THE WILDERNESS"**, PRIMITIVE WILDERNESS LIVING & SURVIVAL SKILLS, is a compilation of ten individual booklets, each covering a primitive skill in depth. The purpose of them was, and is, to teach the complete novice "how-to" do "things" for themselves. To say that they are successful is an understatement. Since 1986, over 150,000 of the small books have been printed - and over 14,000 of the larger compilation since 1993. This with no publisher. Just us and word of mouth for the most part. Videos that we have done on some of the subject/chapters have also sold into the thousands.

I don't mention this here to impress anyone - you've already bought this - only to impress the fact that there is a multitude of people out there searching for something that they can do for themselves. What we wrote works. We've had thousands of pieces of correspondence and phone calls from folks saying so. And, they wanted more.

Well, we kinda figured that the compilation was pretty much complete in illustrating all the *skills* that one would need to head to the wilderness - not that one would - just kinda nice knowing that you knew. Therefore the title, **"Naked into the Wilderness"**. Sure, we have learned more about the skills since the publication of the book - but not enough to justify another volumn. So what next?

Doin' it.

Many, both beginners and those who have become adept with these skills, have no idea of just how and where they might fit them in today. (Chapter 6 gives a pretty in depth look as to our feelings on this.)

Book #1 took right at eight years to compile and put together. Some skills we knew enough about at the start to write about. Others we had to hone. One, pottery, we pretty much had to learn from scratch. But we got it together, photographing step by step and passing it on to you. This book took only three years - and while we have been *doing* for years, putting them into a book wasn't on our minds. Fortunately we took notes and photos.

Chapter one deals with what should be a top priority in primitive skills ... hantavirus. The lifestyle of primitive living just about requires trapping to succeed ... and the bread and butter from those traps is, and was, rodents ... the very carriers of this deadly disease. And while we're on the subject of eating, in **chapter two** we give our reasons why one cannot realistically be a vegetarian in a primitive or survival situation for an extended period.

Back to skills. **Chapter three** delves into hair-on brain tanning. The first book that we published, back in 1986, was on brain tanning. From the start people wanted to jump into robes, mostly buffalo. Here we do a deer robe and a bobcat pelt.

As mentioned, we have been working on various projects over the past several years, many with some local (loco) youngsters. After touching on the basics of primitive living one year, a 9'x17' grass house done the second (all with stone tools), the third summer it was decided by them to tackle something more challenging, a dugout canoe - done with stone tools. So, this is **chapter four**.

Chapter five is going to be where I stick anything that I think needs to be stuck somewhere, stuff that has no specific heading or enough material to deserve its own chapter.

Chapter six thru **nine** (also chapter one) were originally written as articles for the **WILDERNESS WAY** magazine (POB 203, Lufkin, TX 75902-0203). We retained the copyright so as to include them here. Six are our thoughts on primitive today. Seven, eight and nine are three sequential days of a trip "Naked into the Wilderness" (with clothes) here in Kansas - actually right in our own back forty.

Chapter ten. Five years in the making. This is a short story based on characters and scenes from a novel that Geri just finished and is now in search of a publisher - other than ourselves. Our plans from the beginning were to self-publish this as we have our other works ... hell, we got *the* audience ... but Geri's profes sor at KSU (she knew *what* she wanted to say, just not *how*), after four years on and off of reading and helping her along, feels that she would do herself and others a better service by going thru his agent, at least for a reference, to a real publisher. Big time!

You'll notice while reading thru this that I keep refering to *I* and *we*. Well, I, John, do most all of the "how-to" *writing*. Geri is there at every step when I yell "help". The skills, we are *both* always doing.

John & Geri McPherson
Sept. 1996
Randolph, Kansas

Chapter
1

HANTAVIRUS
Pulmonary Syndrome

*W*hen it comes to any study of primitive living skills, trapping is a necessary subject. We firmly believe that trapping was, and is, responsible for the majority of sustenance in any sort of survival or primitive living effort.

Plants can be gathered in everyday movements with a minimal of effort in many cases - but also a minimal return of essential nutrients and calories (as noted in several other places in this book). Time spent hunting, in our opinion, is time better spent on other living projects using the hunting tools for opportunistic moments.

Traps will catch and hold just about any form of animal life from fish to insects to deer sized game ... but by far the major source of sustenance will come from small rodent sized animals. Consuming all or most parts of these quarry will supply most or all of the nutrients and calories necessary for the human body to not only survive but to thrive.

Since 1993 there have been 138 confirmed instances in the United States of a viral disease, *hantavirus pulmonary syndrome* (HPS) which has a very high mortality rate.

The host for this virus? Rodents.

The first reports came from the four corners area of the southwest. Several persons on the Navajo Indian Reservation died suddenly. It seems that many of the infected people had been collecting pinon nuts - stored conveniently for them in caches by rodents, most notably deer mice. There had been a hearty crop of the pinon nut - which led to a heavier than normal population of deer mice - caused, some theorize, by unseasonably heavy rains.

Whatever, the deer mouse was pinpointed as the source.

Since then there have been cases of HPS reported in 24 states: all of the west, part of the southeast into Florida, up into the northeast into New York and Rhode Island and into Canada.

Hey folks, that's like saying that the entire country has it.

Various hantaviruses are known throughout the world (the name coming from a river in Korea) and there are several distinct viruses (or species). Those lucky enough to contact it in Europe have only a 1% chance of dying ... in Asia this is upped to 15%. The strains in the Americas are much more lethal. When first reported the mortality was a whopping 70% but

> ••• *the mortality was a*
> *whopping 70%*
> *but has since dropped to about*
> *50%* •••

has since dropped to about 50%, probably because of better communication and awareness of medical personnel. The higher fatality rate comes from the fact that in the American strain (HPS), the lungs rapidly fill with fluid.

The range of the primary carrier, the deer mouse, covers most all of the U.S. and tests on them have shown the virus to be throughout most of its range. Other carriers are the cotton rat (Florida), rice rat (Southeast), white footed mouse (Northeast) the pinon mouse and the Western chipmunk. A carrier of the not so dangerous Seoul virus (distributed worldwide) is the Norway rat. The infected rodents exhibit no visible symtoms.The list, both of viruses and of carriers, has expanded since '93 . Human cases of HPS have been positively identified in the U.S. as early as 1978 and inferred back to 1959.

In all cases to date, victims were infected by coming into contact with feces, urine or saliva of infected rodents. Since the virus is in the body fluids it can be assumed that it is throughout the body. Most cases reportedly were a result of *breathing the dust* of disturbed feces, saliva and/or urine of infected rodents.

> ***If your hands come in contact with anything that is contaminated and then reach your mouth or nose, there is a chance of infection.***

The survival time in the environment is unknown. Periods of up to two days on a dried surface is suggested. If your hands come in contact with anything that is contaminated and then reach your mouth or nose, there is a chance of infection. You can also get it by being bitten by an infected rodent.

So far there is no evidence that it can be transmitted from person to person or from insects (such as fleas).

The virus is easily killed with most general purpose household disinfectants (bleach, alcohol). In other words, if you got a lot of nests, feces, etc. in your woodpile, shed or outhouse it would be best to spray it down with a disinfectant prior to cleaning it up. A 1% (1:100) dilution of household bleach for wiping down potentially contaminated surfaces and a more concentrated dilution of 10% is suggested for heavily contaminated areas such as nest sites. A new solution should be mixed daily.

Just how concerned should one be? Well, of deer mice tested in three counties of Western Kansas in 1993, 9% were infected. We live in North central KS so that's getting pretty close to home.

> *You don't have to stick your head*
> *in a bucket of mouse scat and*
> *take a deep breath to become infected.*
> *One sniff is all that it takes.*

You don't have to stick your head in a bucket of mouse scat and take a deep breath to become infected. One sniff is all that it takes. This means that something as mundane as moving the woodpile, with the accompanying mice and packrat nests, becomes hazardous. A little mathematics. Using 9% as the baseline, if there is one mouse nest in the pile, there is a 9% chance that it is infected. Two, 18%. If among all the wood we move around here there are nine nests, there is a 100% chance that we will come into contact with HPS. If infected, there is a 50% chance of dying from it. That don't sound like good odds to me.

For clean-up of rodent contaminated areas, the Centers for Disease Controls (CDC) recommends the complete wetting down of the area with a disinfectant, wearing of an approved respirator (in enclosed spaces with heavy, active rodent infestations), wearing of rubber gloves, washing of the rubber gloves with a disinfectant when finished, followed by the washing of

> *... prompt medical attention is a must to increase the chances of survival.*

your hands and burying or burning of the any suspected materials. Whew!

Symptoms are flu-like: fever, muscle aches, abdominal, joint and lower back pain, headaches, cough, nausea, vomiting and diarrhea. If any of these symptoms are exhibited for up to six weeks after possible exposure, seek help immediately. Since there is no known curative drug, prompt medical attention is a must to increase the chances of survival.

How does this effect us primitives? Let me tell

> *This is serious business.*
> *One touch or sniff is all that it takes.*

you that Geri and I don't mess with mice and packrats anymore. This is serious business. One touch or sniff is all that it takes. Recommended precautions for campers and hikers, besides the obvious steps of avoiding contact with nests or burrows, includes not sleeping directly on the ground ... as natural as making cordage for us. Mice pee everywhere they go leaving a scent trail - sleeping on the ground increases the risks of your breathing this.

Trapping, like friction fire making, ranks right up there at the top of the primitive's priority list. Can, or even should we discontinue this practice?

Knowledge, awareness, caution and weighing of the facts of the personal risks by each individual is in order.

We still teach and write about the importance of traps ... and also how in a *real* survival or primitive situation that one may have to depend on some rodents. We have to. Primitive, primitive living and survival demand this knowledge. In a survival situation the risks must be weighed ... the human body can go several weeks without any food at all. But we stress staying away from the mice and other listed carriers if, and when, possible. Each individual has to make his or her own decisions.

Hey, the list has grown continually. What was considered safe yesterday just might not be today - or tomorrow.

Suspect all rodents. Put off limits those that are for sure hosts of this deadly virus. Pack, or wood rats are not on the list ... yet. So what does one do if you catch one? Or a squirrel? A muskrat? Weigh the facts and the situation.

19

Heat kills. HPS is a fragile virus. If all portions of the rodent is subjected to a high enough temperature, the disease is killed. The safest way that we have come up with to handle this would be to, #1, *not handle with the hands*. Shove a stick in its mouth or butt - be careful of any blood or other fluids. Singe the hair off, scrape with another stick (burn the sticks - try not to inhale the smoke) and place the critter directly in the coals. Or boil it. Or roast in a makeshift oven. Fry it on a flat, hot rock. Whatever, don't handle the animal until it has been well cooked ... until the meat is not pink ... and thensome. 140° F (160° better yet) for at least 20

> *The danger lies not so much in the cooking and eating as in the handling prior to.*

minutes. (This message comes to us direct from the CDC.)

Carrying the suspect animal in a basket will require the burning of the basket. The danger lies not so much in the cooking and eating as in the handling prior to. A rock or log falling on an animal is enough to literally squeeze the pee outta him ... breathing *that* can infect you. Use caution!

I wish to acknowledge Michael H. Bradshaw and Liz Boyle; Extension Specialists at Kansas State

University, and Lori Miller and Kristi Busico of the
Centers for Disease Control in Atlanta, Ga for their
help in obtaining information contained in this chapter.
When I first contacted them they were kind of at a loss
for answers pertaining to HPS and the eating of mice.
It just wasn't one of the areas that they study. The up to
date information presented here was done with their
help.

A fact sheet (MF-1117) can be obtained from
the Cooperative Extension Service, Kansas State
University, Manhattan, KS 66531. Information can
also be obtained by calling the CDC in Atlanta at 800/
532-9929 or writing the Dept. of Health and Human
Services, Public Health Service, CDC, Atlanta, GA
30333

•

Addendum: On 19 September '96 there was
reported a second death attributed to hantavirus in a
two week period in Western Kansas. The first was
contacted while cleaning a basement.

Chapter 2

NUTRITION

FOR

THE PRIMITIVE

> ••• *BE SURE TO READ CHAPTER 1 ON HANTAVIRUS BEFORE ATTEMPTING TO TRAP RODENTS!* •••

1 - **The human being cannot be a vegetarian in the wilderness under primitive conditions** (with the possible exception of in the tropics).

2 - **All nutrients required to keep the human body alive can be found in the animal kingdom.**

3 - **In reality, it is a combination of plants and animals that supply the necessary nutrients to keep primitives alive.**

*L*et me begin by saying that *food is secondary in importance to water in any situation* - so bear this in mind as you read on. I'll cover water a bit in the final paragraphs of this chapter.

Also, tho it may at times not appear so in this discussion, both Geri and I could easily be vegetarians except that we both like to eat meat. We are not knocking vegetarians here ... only saying that in an *extended* primitive wilderness living or survival situation it is not possible to live vegetarian.

•

Every stage, path or platform of primitive technology relates in some manner to plants. In fact, besides stone and animal parts, it is all plant orientated ... and the animal part is a result of plants in some manner (cordage & wood in hunting and trapping).

As far back as I can remember, whenever one spoke of outdoor living, the subject of edible plants arose. What I want to discuss here is how plants are ... and more importantly to us, ... *are not* ... related to primitive living as a food source.

The thought is prevalent among pursuers of the primitive life-style that by taking a hike in the wilderness, pointing to a plant, mumbling Latin and saying that such and such part if harvested at a particular time of the year, prepared in such and such a way (making certain that one doesn't confuse it with a certain look-a-

23

like plant that just might turn one's insides to jelly), can supply a certain percentage of one's daily allowance of vitamin such and such.

Sound confusing? Part of the point I'm trying to make.

Plants are essential to primitive living - always have been and always will be. But, you will die trying to be a vegetarian in the wilderness. Our contention is

> ### ... *the human body will thrive by following an all animal product diet* ...

that the human body will thrive, getting all the nutrients and calories necessary, with a minimum of training, by following an all animal product diet ... and after years of training in edible and medicinal plants one will not get by nearly as well and will most likely die after an extended period if one relies solely on plants for food.

If it's living a primitive life-style that you are looking for, skills is what you will want to learn.

The dictionary defines abstract: 1) "as having no material existence. 2) Theoretical rather than practical."

If you wanta make a fire, learn which sticks and in what manner to use them - reality. Not how to communicate with the trees so that they will tell you how to do it - abstract.

24

If you want to fill your belly - regularly - and
with a minimal of effort and a minimal of training - and

> *A trap can be learned in*
> *half an hour or less. A days practice*
> *will make you proficient with it.*

with the right stuff that will maintain and build your
body - and thrive, not just survive, over any extended
period of time, learn to trap animals and eat what you
catch. The trap can be learned in half an hour or less. A
days practice will make you proficient with it. Learning
where to set a trap will take just a bit longer.

The hard part of it will be to learn what parts of
an animal are not good to eat ... for example, some
livers, especially of carniverous animals, may have a
toxic amount of vitamin A ... (much simpler than
learning the same about plants). A tour of the innards of
an animal will show what to look for as far as healthy
goes. Unhealthy livers are the main thing to keep an eye
out for besides obvious cancerous sores interior and
exterior. Whatever, learning this information will take
you only days; a few visits to the library ... talks with a
veterinarian or a medical doctor ... a visit to the local
locker plant for a show and tell with the butcher and/or
state inspector. Not a real chore.

Learning plants, on the other hand, what can and
cannot be eaten, is such a long term project that I

hesitate to limit it to years.

> **Nurturing our bodies is realistic.**
> **Doing so safely with a minimum of effort is**
> **practical.**

Over the years we have found that the folks that have been following our writings are looking for practical and realistic ways to turn part of their lives into a natural experience - the key words here are *practical* and *realistic*.

Nurturing our bodies is realistic. Doing so safely with a minimum of effort is practical.

Don't get me wrong. I have respect for those who have devoted a major portion of their lives to learning, understanding and passing on any and all sorts of plant information, whether edible or medicinal.

> **To be an expert all 'round primitive**
> **outdoorsperson, one needs to be**
> **proficient in an entire circle of skills.**

I just get tired of hearing of what a wilderness expert so and so is _because_ of his ability of touring a woodlot, pointing, nibbling, mumbling Latin and saying how wonderful it is to be "one" with nature. Never mind that the so called expert may not be able to make a fire by friction, tools, shelter, cordage, containers, or traps

... all from the materials at hand. To be an expert all 'round primitive outdoorsperson, one needs to be proficient with an entire circle of skills. You can't make a primitive pot to cook your foods in without being able to make a primitive fire.

The human body requires the intake of several nutrients to stay alive. **Fats, carbohydrates**, and **protein** are the big three. This is where the calories, or fuel, comes from. Many **vitamins, minerals** and **amino & fatty acids** combine to make this a pretty long list.

Energy comes from calories ... not vitamins and minerals. Calories come from fats, carbohydrates and protein. Fats have about 9 (twice as many) calories per gram versus 4 per gram for carbs and protein. Calories are more co-efficient from carbs than from protein. Simply put, the body utilizes calories derived from carbohydrates more efficiently than it does those from protein - and you get twice as much energy from fat.

A lack of calories will kill you in the short haul. A deficiency of vitamins, minerals and the essential acids will get you in the long haul.

It's kinda complicated (I'm trying my best to keep it simple) but some of the vitamins, minerals and acids are *made within* the body from food sources. Others, such as vitamin C, B-complex and several "essential" amino acids are not. These must be ingested.

A resting body requires a certain input of energy (calories) to sustain life. I, John, require right at 2,000 calories a day for my resting, unstressed 5' 10", 155 lb frame just to maintain (2,500 is considered average). A moving, working or stressed body requires more. Take in less than what is required and the body withers and dies. Take in more and it is stored as fat. (The for sure "wonder" diet is to do more than you eat.) What is taken in is sorted (in the stomach, intestines and internal organs) - the good kept and the waste eliminated. Properties change (carbohydrates {starches} become sugar and/or fat depending on the need of the body at the moment). Vitamins, minerals and acids are absorbed and put where needed.

So, a simple list.
1 - Fat
2 - Protein
3 - Carbohydrates
4 - Vitamins
5 - Minerals
6 - Acids (essential, amino, fatty) - all
add up to ...
Calories (energy) *and* **nutrients**
necessary to sustain human life.

If we burn more energy in gathering and preparing the energy listed above than what we take in, we die.

If we gather the total amount of energy (calories), or even more than what we need and it does not include all of components (nutrients) that our body requires, we die.

It's really pretty simple. It might take three months but there are many recorded instances of folks dying with full bellies.

> *There are many recorded instances of folks dying with full bellies.*

So just what is the most practical and realistic method of fulfilling our bodily requirements in a primitive and/ or survival situation?

PLANTS

Look at any book dealing with edible plants. All that I have ever seen (and there are many in our library) list hundreds. In the past I have seriously delved into some of them to try to become a better "all 'round woodsman". Literally hundreds of listings! Talk about overwhelmed. I had no idea where to begin. I knew nothing about plants - therefore the books. Lots of warnings of dangerous look-alikes. Most had no photos,

> *If conditions are right,*
> *you can live for weeks with*
> *no intake of nutrients at all.*

just drawings. Looking at a drawn rendition and maybe the real thing just don't cut it with us. I've never seen a book describing the nutritional value of all of the plants. Most list none. Many have warnings to never try anything before being shown for sure by someone who knew. Needless to say I haven't seen what I would call a good book on plant identification.

OK, lets get beyond that for a moment. Lets say you know plants. You know them well. You've got several years of identifying, gathering and preparing behind you. You even know the calories provided and nutritional value of a goodly assortment. If placed in a true primitive environment or survival situation, I still say that you will die from starvation and/or malnutrition. Not overnight for sure. It can take months for the body to wither from lack of nutrients. If conditions are right, you can live for weeks with no intake of foods at all.

Anecdote ... *the poor, ignorant kid who died slowly over, I believe it was 118 days in Alaska a few years back. Kept a diary to tell us about it. Had a pack full of goodies: matches, .22 caliber rifle, sleeping bag,* *book on edible plants. Huh? did you read that right? Yep!, he had his book on edible plants. His diary told us how he got lost. Hurt his leg somehow. He found an abandoned school bus for shelter. He left notes telling anyone who came along that he was out gathering berries - it was springtime. His diary tells us what a mistake he made in shooting a moose with his .22. It was rotting in just a few days ... filled with maggots. So he let this entire source of nutrients rot away and looked for berries. Kept getting weaker and weaker till he died.*

We received a copy of a news article on this several years back from a friend asking if anything in our writings could have saved him - *yes, chapter 4* of our first Naked into the Wilderness book.

But lets say you got lost here in the richness of N.E. Kansas. We got it all here. Lets say you began your primitive survival trip in the spring when plants are coming into their own. Now because of my lack of knowledge of plants I can't say just what the specific seasons are, but plants do have their seasons. One example would be the magic acorn. The acorn has lots. Fats, protein and carbohydrates. Plus many of the vitamins, minerals and acids. But ... they ain't ready until the fall ... and then you gotta be quick to get 'em ahead of the squirrels. Certain plants, jerusalem artichoke is one we've been told of, have to sit thru the winter before the tubers are worth digging for nutrients. Just begin to imagine the knowledge that you'll need. Not only do you have to be able to identify plants as they are growing but also after they have withered down to nothing. Whew!!!

Now if a really good plant specialist, **and also** a really good all 'round expert primitive technologist were to exist (I think I might know *one* - note the think and might), I just might listen to their argument that he/ she could become <u>close</u> to a vegetarian *after a years worth of gathering and preserving,* meanwhile existing on a diet comprised of plant and animal products. At least one element, vitamin B-12, *is found only in animal products.*

> *Shelter, fire, clothing ,water, containers, cooking vessels ... all of this stresses the body and burns calories.*

Remember, when placed in a primitive survival environment, food is not the only concern. Shelter, fire, clothing if necessary, water, containers, cooking vessels are just a few of the things one needs to concern themselves with. All of this stresses the body and burns calories. Add to this the energy required in the gathering of food. It don't take much figuring to see that plants alone just won't take care of the situation.

One lady once wrote us convinced that all she

had to do was chew on grass, swallow the juices, spit out the stems and she would get along fine. I mean she really believes this. It's just that sort of garbage that will continue to kill the unwary outdoorsperson.

ANIMAL PRODUCTS

Note that I say animal *products*, not just meat. One can starve to death on meat alone the same as grass. The list of nutrients earlier are just as valid here. It's just that with animals, all the nutrients are there along with a sufficient amount of calories. All in one neat little package. You just gotta eat it all. And if, by

> *With animals, all the nutrients are there along with a sufficient amount of calories. All in one neat little package. You just gotta eat it all.*

chance, not every essential amino acid is present in one animal, it might well be in the next.

The fact is that animals will provide everything that the body requires. If you want, ***and you should***, supplement with plants, not out of necessity but simply for the variety. In this case you don't hafta know anything at all about the nutritional value of any particular plant, only that it's safe to eat. Cattails, burdock, yucca flower and leaf. Acorns and nuts. Grass seeds. A short simple list, easy to learn and remember - but not at all necessary because *the animal has it all.*

Some information from the Kansas State University Cooperative Extension Service.

One chart lists, among other things, protein, fat and energy of various meats (just meat). I'll leave beef and other domesticated animals out of this discussion. Various deer, elk, rabbits and many birds made up the remaining 19 on this list. The protein (g/100g) ranged from 21.4 (squirrel) to 25.7 (wild pheasant). The fat ran from a low of 0.5 (g/100g) of moose to a high of 25.7 (g/100g) for wild turkey. Calories ... (Kcal/100g) ... 121 for the snow goose, 163 for the wild turkey and a whopping 255 for the raccoon. Additional charts provided for these and other wild animals gave impressive listings of nutrients.

Let me list here what the roasted meat of the raccoon contains per 100g; Calories - 255, Protein - 29.2g, fat - 14.5g, ash, Thiamin-B1, Riboflavin-B2, Niacin-B3, Vitamin B6, Vitamin B12, Vitamin D, Vit E-Alpha, Copper, Iron, Magnesium, Phosphorus, Potassium, Sodium, and Zinc. That's 17, count 'em, 17 different elements in **just the meat**. Plus 255 calories. Other elements obtained from other wild meat sources included retinol, carotenoid, vitamin C, calcium, manganese and selenium. *Much more is gleaned when you eat the various internal organs and break the bones*

34

open for the nutritionally rich marrow.

One trap. One 'coon. Minimal effort expended for a highly nutritious return. The average racoon weights in at around 22 to 25 pounds. To be liberal subtract one third to arrive at what you will be eating ... lets say 15 pounds. Now figuring the least nutritious part of this 15 lbs., the meat, it will take just over two pounds of roasted raccoon meat to provide 2,500 calories. Being very liberal, with the meat alone being figured, this one raccoon will sustain us for six days. And it, or its equivilant, *is available at any time of the year.* Excess meat can be dried and preserved indefinitely (see chapter 4 of our previous book).

A raccoon sized animal is medium sized and really not that difficult to trap. The daily bread and butter would be smaller rodents **(again, do read chapter 1 on hantavirus)**. Animals the size of deer or even moose can be trapped with a bit more effort. Remember tho that this trapping is in most cases illegal today except in real survival situations.

A good example of man sustaining himself on an animal only diet can be made from the life of arctic explorer Vilhjalmur Stefansson. Born in Canada in the late 1800's, he subsisted on an animal only diet for a good portion of his life. In the mid 1920's he had lived over ten continous years on a mostly mcat only dict. An experiment was carried out on him and another explorer in 1927-28 where the two ate nothing but an all animal diet for one year - the first six months under observation in a hospital. Their health at the end of the experiment was the same as at the beginning. Stefansson died at the age of 82.

> ### *Animals is where it's at when it comes to sustenance.*

The point being made here is that animals is where it's at when it comes to sustenance. Use plants when and where the opportunity arises according to your knowledge and the availability of them, ... but don't depend on them alone for any long term survival.

A recent associated press article is of interest. To fight malnutrition among the poor, health oficials in Brazil began production in 1990 of an experimental food supplement called Prothemol. Cow blood, containing eight essential amino acids, is the core of the product with dried egg white, vitamin A and flour added. The blood was discovered to be even more nutritious than the meat. The only complaint to date was the fact that the children were growing so fast that clothes had to be replaced more often.

Trapping is the way to go in the primitive survival situation. The traps that take minutes to make and set are working for you while you are building a shelter, making fire, gathering, cording, etc. Hunting by itself should be considered opportunistic at best. Many,

many hours can be spent trying to hunt something, taking away the time that could be better spent on other survival or long term primitive living tasks.

Water

The human body is by weight composed of close to 70% water ... and tho not really a nutrient as per our discussion here, the body cannot survive without it. This subject is much deeper than the scope of this chapter so we won't delve too deeply into it.

The body constantly loses water thru defecation, urination, sweating and even breathing. This has to be replaced. As little as a 2% drop of the bodies water supply can lead to a 20% loss in mental and muscular activity. The inactive individual will die in 7 days or less in 90° F if none is replaced - sooner if one is injured or stressed. At 70° F, two to three quarts a day is required to maintain a normal level -*doing nothing*.

The primitive of old had only the concern of finding water - and when he did it was usually potable. Not so today. Finding a source of pure drinking water is the exception rather than the rule. In days gone by the main worry of the primitive was that something was decaying upstream from where she was taking a drink. The smart primitive of today don't drink from open waters. Springs, for the most part seem to provide safe drinking water - but even then many of the underground reservoirs are poluted by various chemicals.

There are many and various techniques of obtaining and purifying water but most all are not "primitive". Many modern survival books deal well with this subject.

I pulled eight books dealing with edible wild plants from our library and looked up cattail - about the most commonplace and well known of all the edible wild plants that is touted by all outdoorspersons. The plant is listed in all eight. Seven of those eight give no nutritional facts for the cattail. Two of them mention the word starch in conjunction with.

Only one, a small, non-descript paperback called "Eat the Weeds", by Ben Charles Harris, copyrighted in 1961, impressed me at all with its description stating that it is reported to contain protein, sulphur, phosphorus, carbohydrates, sugar and oils in flour derived from it, especially the pollen. Now that's usable information!

He gives the nutritional values of many of the 150 or so plants he describes. Unfortunately this book has no photos or even drawings of the plants covered.

A special thanx to Elizabeth Boyle; Extension Specialist at Kansas State University for her assistance in providing information and guidance with this chapter.

The readily identified, edible at all seasons, cattail.

Chapter
3

Brain Tanning
Robes and Furs

Geri wearing Eskimo style parka made from four deer robes.

Our first book, Brain Tan Buckskin, was published in the spring of 1986. Immediately people began writing asking about tanning skins with the hair left on. I mean, like everyone was wanting to tackle a buffalo robe. After about the third printing I added a short summary on the necessary steps to do this.

Leaving the hair on buckskin seems at first as simple as not taking it off. Maybe even a time and labor saving step. Not so! For reasons that will become clear shortly, the time and work loads will increase consider

Geri prepares to soak up buffalo which turned out to be unusable. Yeah, it's cold out.

ably - many times by a factor more than ten. Lots, and I mean lots, of extra work and time is involved. The bigger and thicker the skin/hide, the more this factor increases - (thinner coyotes might have the factor only double).

How about some terminology.

Pelt - outside of fur bearing animals.

Skin - outside of non-fur bearing animals up to the size of deer.

Hides - outside of animals larger than deer.

Coyotes have pelts, deer skins and cow, buffalo and moose hides. A tanned coyote with the hair left on is a pelt. A tanned deer or moose with hair left on is a robe.

Coyotes have fur. Deer, elk and moose have hair. Buffalo, sheep and llamas have wool.

What we're gonna do here is tan a deer robe and a bobcat pelt. We had planned to do a buffalo for this chapter but the hide that we had was cut and scored so badly in skinning that it is completely unusable. The only thing we have on hand of any size is the deer.

When I wrote the book **Brain Tan Buckskin**, I made the statement that tanning deer-like animals with the hair on was kind've a waste of time as the hairs, being hollow, tend to break off easily. Well, since then we have tanned one elk and several deer robes. Was all we had. So call me a liar. The hair still breaks off. Now ten years later, I sit in almost the exact same spot (seven feet higher and maybe three off to the side) giving instruction on how to do this.

•

The following summary was written as a supplement to the book (chapter) on brain tanning buckskin. We reccommend that you tan a buckskin or two before tackling a robe ... but whatever, tho the following is addressed to those readers of our first book it is of equal importance to include here.

BRIEF, ALL IMPORTANT, SUMMARY
So pay attention!

What I describe here may not actually be the scientific facts that some are searching for...but if you understand what is put forth here you will know what is happening to the skin...*and why*. This knowledge will not only help you to better approach the task at hand, but will also be invaluable in troubleshooting and correcting mistakes. First you must understand the product which you are working with, the skin.

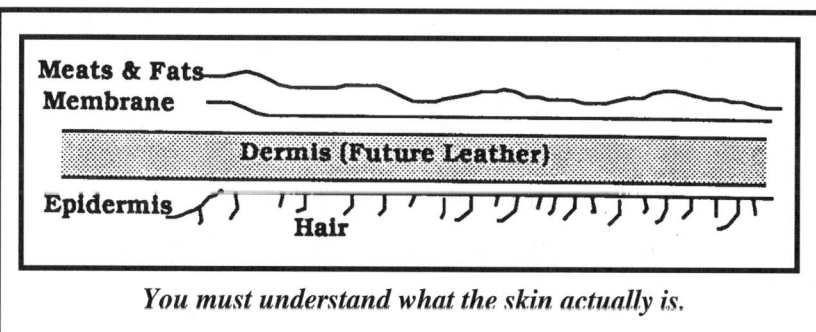

You must understand what the skin actually is.

The future leather (the dermis) is actually millions of tiny threads. You **MUST** visualize this ... think of it as very compressed cotton. An inherent

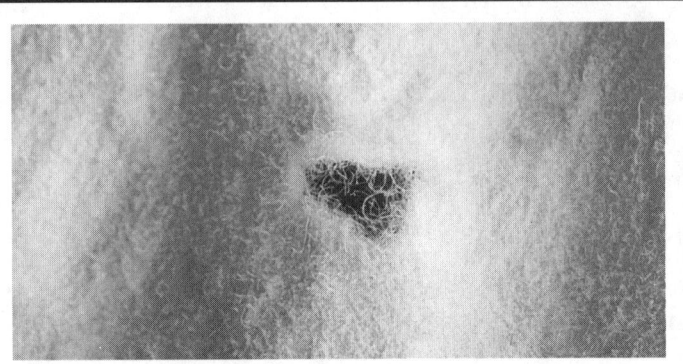

An important point to comprehend is that the skin is composed of millions of fibers - these loose fibers are brain tanned buffalo.

property of these threads is glue. Boil them down and you have hide glue. Oils, in our case from the brains, (lOW motor oil might work ... Ivory soap does ... just not as well as brains) are penetrated COMPLETELY through the dermis to coat all of these threads. In the methods illustrated here, the brains (oils) are mixed with water ... water is thinner than the oils and therefore penetrates easier and faster ... BUT ... the <u>oils will not penetrate through the membranes</u> sandwiching either side of the skin. Water will. Oils won't. Therefore the necessity of removing these membranes. The inner membrane, which is a solid sheet, is easily removed, most times completely, while fleshing. Sandpaper will show where this has been missed. The outer membrane, the epidermis, is no harder nor more or less important to remove than the inner ... BUT ... it is the hardest for you to LEARN to remove. The epedermis is not a solid sheet ... in fact it more compares to sandpaper, millions of tiny dots ... the *grain* of leather. This is removed, in our method, by dry scraping - removing the hair and the epidermis at the same time. Your scraper will remove hair <u>and</u> epidermis from an area about 1/4 inch wide each lick ... work an area about 1 inch wide ... overlap your strokes ... let your eyes penetrate *into* the skin ... you will eventually see what you are removing. It DOES NOT look the same all over the skin. It may take 10 to 12 strokes before you have successfully removed the epidermis from your 1 inch wide strip. PAY AT-TENTION!

Once the surfaces are prepared, the oils will be able to penetrate. We need to coat EVERY fiber with these oils ... therefore repeated applications ... you cannot overbrain. But, once oiled, if left unattended, the skin will shrink and dry hard (the glue taking effect) ... but, if you are to MOVE THESE LUBRICATED FIBERS UPON THEMSELVES while the skin dries, the oils will allow the FIBERS TO STAY SEPA-RATED AND THEY WILL SWELL SOMEWHAT ... the result? ... an unbelievably soft flannel-like material. Now if this was to be wetted again, the fibers would again shrink and dry hard (the glue) unless worked. BUT ... if we penetrate the entire, loosely wovenfibered skin with smoke, the pitch will WATERPROOF THE FIBERS. The skin itself is not waterproofed ... water will run through it ... but the *fibers will be water-proofed* ... and the wetted skin will again dry soft since the water has not been allowed to get to the INDI-VIDUAL FIBERS and allow the glue to take effect. Once you understand this, you are in control. (I became aware of the glue action above mentioned thru Jim Rigg's book *"Blue Mountain Buckskin"*)

STEPS FOR TANNING A DEER ROBE

The stages you will be taken through here are the same for larger animal hides such as elk and buffalo - except that for those larger animals you will require more - of everything.

STEP	TIME
1- Frame and flesh hide	1.5 hours
2- Sand flesh side	.25 hr.
3- Apply brains	8
4- Manipulating	12
5- Smoking	1
	22.75 total hours

This can be done at one time or spread over as many days as is convenient for you ... however steps #1 and #4 must each be done at one sitting.

MATERIALS

So what might one need in the way of materials for turning out this fine product? Well, not too much. To keep from breaking your back from bending over a skin staked to the ground, we'll first need a ...

Frame. Poles can be lashed and/or nailed together but here we'll use four 2x4's **nailed** or **screwed** double at each corner. Anything larger than a deer will require more sturdy materials. And to lace the skin to the frame we'll need some ...

Cordage of sorts. We pretty much use 1/8th inch nylon cord for our lacing projects as it lasts longer and is plenty strong. Baling twine has been used here as has 1/4" rope. Whatever is handy. For this skin we'll need 4 lengths of about 30 feet each. You'll also need a ...

Knife of sorts to cut the lacing holes and to trim away unwanted areas of the skin. The thinner blades make for smaller holes and this we prefer.

Sandpaper can be used at certain stages - generally a coarse grade of 50 to 60 grit.

Brains, of course. We have used the brains from many animals and all seem to do the job ... *but*. On several occasions we have had problems with not getting enough brain <u>oils</u> into the skins while doing everything else the same except for the fact that we had used beef brains instead of the normal hog brains that we stock up on. No scientific testing here ... just from experience we have found that pigs seem to have more of the oily stuff than do beef. So, if you do use beef brains ... use more. Once we get to finishing this robe out we'll need an additional tool called a ...

Staker. This can be as simple as a heavy, round pointed stick. What we use here is a piece of iron bar because its added weight makes the job here easier.

Some ideas for stakers. What we used here was a wooden pointed stick (top), a pick ax head (middle) and an iron bar (bottom).

A small **stove** of sorts can be handy, but is not necessary for the final step of smoking. The most important tool of all for all 'round tanning is the ...

Scraper. This is a handle of whatever material you choose (the Indians - and us - use Elk antler). My first ever "good" scraper had a handle of heavy osage orange wood. We have found steel strap iron makes the cheapest and best (heavy) handle. The heavier the handle, the less your body has to work. When dry scraping the hair off, this becomes more important. But whatever handle you come up with, attached to it is a blade which we use and illustrate here made of an old

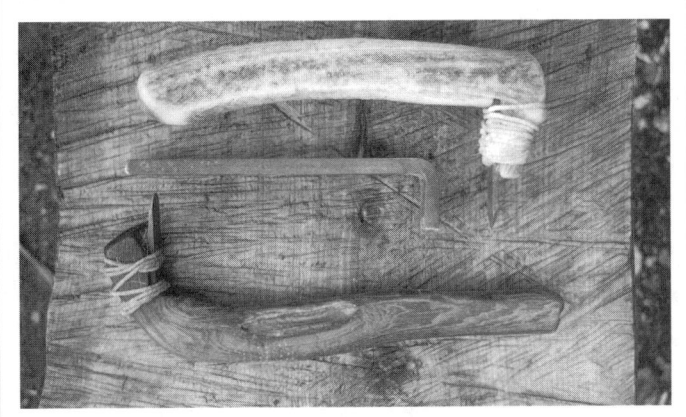

A sampling of handles. Elk antler (top), steel (middle) and wood (bottom). Heavier is better.

(or new) file. The hardness and shaprness of this blade for tanning hair on is not as critical as when de-hairing to make buckskin - but since I'll assume that most wanting to attempt tanning with the hair on will also want to do buckskin (in fact we recommend doing some buckskin first as a learning stage), we'll illustrate here the way to make the blade for that purpose. A duller blade and softer steel can be used for fleshing than for

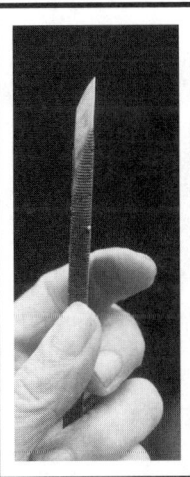 

Side and front view of scraper blade. Size and bevel can vary. Steel shoud be hard so blade will stay sharp longer. This blade is made from an old file - from which we got three - a lifetime supply for most.

dry scrape dehairing.

The length of the handle is not critical. The steel ones that we have had made are ten inches long with another two inches bent at a 90° angle to give a platform to tie the blade to. The elk antler and wood handles are about 15". You will need a platform to tie the blade to of approx. 90° to 110°. It is important that the angle be in this range for the tool to be held properly and give the best cutting edge. At 90° to 100° the base of the handle will pretty much rest on the skin to give the best cutting action to the blade. Too much over 110° and the base of the handle extends out too far to operate comfortably ... too tight of an angle and it just won't bite in at all.

SKINS

Skins are available for the asking. Most deer hunters simply let the locker plant skin the animal and forget about it. The lockers have a ready market to sell them to - but if you approach them during deer season you should have no problems getting one or more for whatever the going price is ... usually around $5.00. I haven't found any hunter that wouldn't jump at the chance to let us skin his deer out ... which for us is much more preferable. Most folks who skin deer do just that - remove the skin or hide. Many feel that the less meat left on the skin the better skinner he is - and this just ain't necessarily so. Skins removed by pulling and pushing the fist between skin and carcass are cleanly removed and well done with no holes or scores (slight cuts into the skin but not deep enough *yet* to be called a hole). When we are in a hurry to get the skin off, such as when we have several to do in a limited time period, we just pull the skin using the knife to cut the thin layer of meat and fat leaving it adhering to the skin. But many skinners get carried away with the knife. Using a knife to skin cleanly is no faster and certainly not better as far as the skin is concerned. Cuts and scores will haunt you later as a lot of stress is placed on the skin in the finishing out stage. The skins of certain animals - usually older and larger - sometimes do require a knife to get them off tho. So I guess that what I'm trying to say here is select as carefully as you can. You'll work just as hard whatever quality the skin - and maybe even harder on the bad ones, and get an inferior product in return. A lot of work is required to brain tan a robe. Choose wisely.

STORAGE

Once you have the skin you'll most likely want to store it for tanning at a later date. The three most common ways to store skins are to freeze, dry or salt. We prefer to freeze all of our skins as when it is time to work it, all we have to do is thaw it out and we have basically what it was when removed from the critter. The drawback to freezing is having to have an energy source (we have no electricity), a freezer or locker space to rent. For several years we rented several drawers at a locker for a reduced rate (they were not in use). Each would keep five to six deer skins depending on how large the package was. We lost that option a coupla years back when they went out of business and now store twelve to fifteen in a freezer located in a neighbors barn several miles from here - good thing that we cut back on our tanning. The skins are wrapped tightly in a bundle with the flesh side in, placed in a plastic garbage bag and sealed by squishing all the air out and tying. Like I mentioned a bit ago, taken out and thawed, it is like working with a fresh skin. They can be stored this way indefinetly. Sometimes skins will become "freezer burned" - this is simply part of a skin that has been exposed to the frozen air - and it has dried out. It appears as a spot (or more commonly as spots) that are swollen and hard. When making buckskin it is more difficult to remove the hair and epidermis from these areas but the finished product doesn't suffer. Leaving the hair on, as here, scrape gently as you approach these spots removing flesh and membranes and you will have no problems.

Salting the skin is the preferred method of preserving for many. Lay the skin out in a shady spot and liberally coat with salt. At its basic, this is all there is to it. We have never employed this method because we have always had access to freezing but we have worked many skins and hides given to us that had been salted. Some folks we know roll the salted skins up, hair side out and allow them to drain. The salt draws the moisture out and should be allowed to drain away as if it pools with the skin it could cause possible hair slippage. We once bought a pile of six buffalo and one steer hide . that had been salted, dried and drained in the shade and then simply piled one on the other. They were about six years old when we got them and except for some minor bug damage they were fine. These salted skins/hides must then be washed well to remove any and all salt and to bring the skin back to its original pliable condition. One advantage to salting the skins is the fact that it seems to help "set" the hair and prevent slippage (the hair "slips" off in bunches if the skin is wetted too long).

Drying the skin is probably the oldest and easiest method of preserving the skin. We have worked with several skins and hides that were simply thrown over a barn rafter, or some such, and left. One elk I tanned (to buckskin) had been in that state for a number of years

Skins can be preserved by simply hanging and drying.

before it was gifted to me by a buddy in Montana. Dried skins, as salted ones, need to be soaked until rejuvenated to their original condition. This can take more than a day but most deer sized skins are ready overnight. Overlong wetting of the skin/hide can cause hair slippage. Soak for the minimum time possible in cool water - preferably in cool weather. A cool running stream would be ideal as a barrel of water can warm quickly, hastening slippage. Another drawback to either of these last two methods is the fact that with the hair and epidermis soaked it will take much longer for them to dry. Place the skin (stretched onto a frame - next section) in a place where it will dry as quickly as possible.

FRAME AND FLESH

We have to now take our skin and lace it into a frame. Not really a difficult job tho many make it out to be so. For the deer skin that we pulled from the freezer - probably about a ten square footer, not big, not small - just a good size to work easily, four seven to eight foot 2x4's will be plenty sturdy for the frame. In fact, the frame that we are using here was one that had already been nailed together for several buckskins and was at the point of falling apart. Only after we had already laced the skin in and fleshed it, did I smarten up enough to take the extra five minutes or so it took to place two screws at each corner for reinforcement. But in order to do it at this stage we had to loosen the now tight skin in the frame so as to be able to get the 2x4's into any semblence of square - and then retighten. So much for doing it right the first time.

Speaking of first time - I'm sure that some of you readers are beginners at this. Those of us who have been doing this sort of thing for many years seem to forget first timers. Simply saying "nail together a frame" just ain't enough for one who has never had a hammer in their hand before - so lets hope that I re- member to get all those little "first timer's hints" that are necessary for a quality "how-to".

Remember, this is not the only way - just our way. I strongly urge anyone doing any skill for the first time to follow one **proven** method or set of rules. We got a call here once from a fellow saying that he was having problems with some step of the brain tanning process.

"John," he say's, "you said to do such and such".

"Yeah," says I.

"Well, he continues, " so and so says to do it this other way in his book. And so and so said to do this."

"Whoa it up," says I. "Get rid of two outta three of those books."

The point I'm trying to make here is that there are several different ways to do these things - and none is better than another if it works for you. But the methods of achieving the end result vary and sometimes conflict. If you try to learn how *we* tan - at the same time comparing it with how Tom & Nancy Oar do it, or Jim Riggs does - or Mel Beattie - well, you're just gonna confuse and frustrate yourself ending with no product at all. Stay with one that works. And this does. Guaranteed.

O.K., so now we've got our fresh, ready to go skin laid out on the ground in front of us. What now? Well, we have a habit here of doing things the same way every time - sometimes one of us might be in the middle of a certain project that just can't be left (like framing and fleshing) and has to leave "right now." The one that has to jump in and pick up can do so more easily if every time things are done the same - so, I'll put to you the way that we do these things.

If the skin is very bloody, you'll want to wash it out. This applies to frozen or fresh skins only as dried or salted will automatically be when soaked. It don't hurt a bit to use some soap or shampoo. We try to avoid the washing if we can because of the danger of hair slippage. With the skin we are working here, things ain't too bad. There is some blood on the hair but we brush this away pretty easily (note photos later in this chapter), using the fingers when necessary to break up stubborn spots. The blood on the flesh side we accept. When doing buckskins this is automatically washed away in the manner that we brain. Leaving the hair on it is not. We will scrape away as much of the blood soaked into the skin as possible - what is left behind will leave hehind a slight darker stain but that will be almost entirely covered when it is smoked. But we're getting a little ahead of ourselves here - this is done after the actual fleshing. Lets get it laced first.

Place the skin, hair down, on the ground. Lay four 2x4's (or whatever), two at the sides first with the top and bottom ones on top. (The reason for placing the boards in this manner is because you may later on have to stand on the bottom one while fleshing and this is much stronger.) Leave about 12 inches of space between the skin and boards and nail securely, twice at each corner. Screwing or bolting will be stronger but for a one time deal, nails are fine. (Actually, this is the only frame that we have ever put together with any-thing but nails over the years.)

Look at the skin and cut off any scraggly bits and pieces hanging on the outskirts. They don't add much to the product but a whole bunch of extra work. If you wanta do something special with the legs and all left on, do it another time after you've gained some experience and can figure out how to work around these hard to do areas. Then take your knife and put holes all around the perimeter of the skin about 2 inches apart, an inch or so in from the edge. You'll make it a lot easier in a bit if you cut and pull away all of the meat, etc from around these holes now.

Spread the skin out and place it in such a manner, hair side down, so that it is slightly closer to the top and right side (as you are facing it) ... neck to the top. Take a length of your cord and run it through a hole at the upper left - that will be in the right side of the deer's neck. This will make it the upper left as you are facing it with the hair side down. Tie this off at the upper left corner of the frame. Take the rest of the cord and run it under the frame out from the skin and over the frame coming back. You *can* do the opposite. Just do them all the same as it will make it simpler when you are repeatedly tightening as you flesh. As you are lacing the top (neck), go through one or two holes at a time. As you

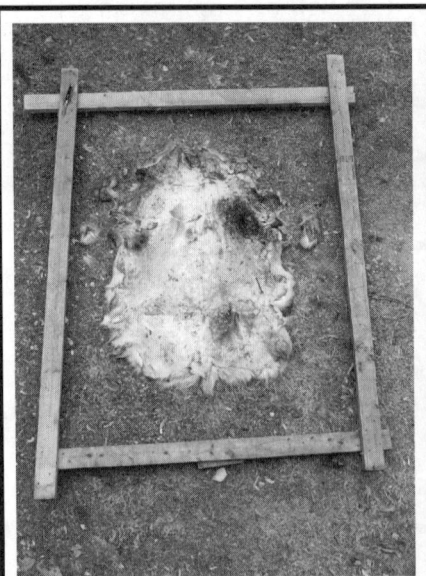

Skin laid within frame (L). Right photo shows how top and bottom are laced in - not stretched outta shape but just kinda pulled towards the top and right side.

reach the other side of the neck, again go through one hole and then around the other corner. Running down the sides make it two or three holes that you run the cord thru. We do 2 or 3 with the rest of the skin as these holes sometimes tear out and if this happens you'll still have the security of another hole or two. The neck is usually strong enough on its own to take the stresses that will be applied.

As you are lacing the top and the right side, don't pull the cords tight. Don't move the skin from its position at all. If you have laid it square in the frame and slightly closer to the top and right side, it will end square. As you reach the bottom right and go around

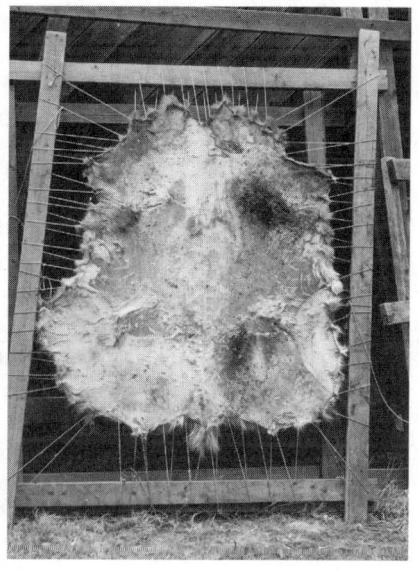

Left photo shows how the skin should look when you've gotten back to the starting point at upper left corner. The right photo shows skin stretched tight to begin fleshing. If all skins are laced this way they will automatically assume their natural shape.

that corner, *then* begin to put tension on the cord ... all across the bottom and then especially while going up the left side. Be careful at the bottom because, even though it will turn out as strong as the rest of the skin, it is now the weakest and the holes will tear out easily. Just snug it for now. By the time you reach the top you should have used most of the four lengths of cord - and the skin should be square and somewhat tight in the frame. Stand it up against something and retighten it all. For the fleshing it needs to be good'n'tite.

As I mentioned earlier, this is one of the stages that has to be done at one sitting. If the skin dries out, it becomes impossible to flesh. Keep a bottle or bucket of water handy to keep it wet. Take the scraper - I prefer it sharp, Geri dull - and begin at the top. Remove the meats, fats and membrane. Once you get it started it's pretty simple. You'll find that a sidewards slicing motion will be needed across much of the top to *open* the flesh from the skin. Once started, it is easy to clean what you don't want from what you do. What you don't want is anything that ain't skin (dermis) - meats, fats and membrane. The membrane will be the trickiest for you to understand until you do one skin. Place your finger on the clean skin and if it stays firm as you try to gently slide it, you've done your job (place your finger on a piece of wood and the feeling is the same). If something slides under your finger between the skin and you - kinda slimy like, that's membrane. Get it off.

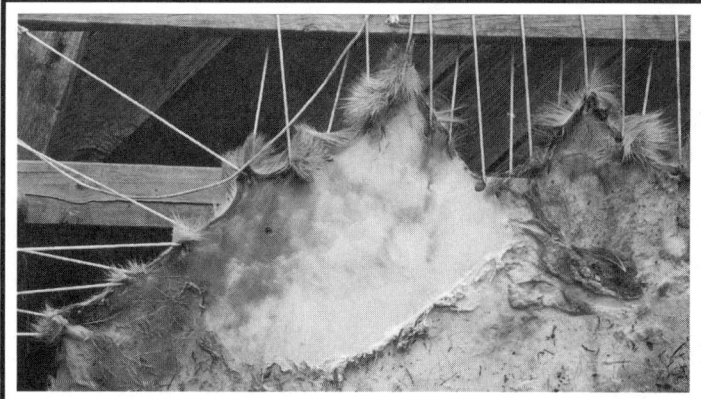

Begin by removing the flesh, membrane and fats from the top (neck).

The membrane can be mostly taken off during skinning if you take your time while "fisting". You'll find that at the legs it will seem to spread out, kinda in layers. These will be the hardest places to get it off. Work the scraper towards the outside here to make it easier. We

These two photos kinda give you an illustration of how the rounded scraper blade works behind *the flesh and membrane to efficiently remove them.*

generally scrape straight down the middle of the skin and then tackle the sides by scraping outwards.

On the bigger, older bucks you might find yourself having a time in the neck area as it really wants to stick there. And be careful with a sharp scraper as it's possible to cut into the skin itself - something you don't want to do. It can be as bad as scoring. Once you get it clean all over, go back and work around the lacing. It can be a pain, but if you get it clean, you can soften it all the way to the edge. By fleshing on a beam you can eliminate this extra as the skin gets clean to the

Geri finishes cleaning up the skin while Smoke patiently waits for his treat.

very edge but it is an extra piece of equipment and another tool. We don't do it that way here.

Once good and clean, leave it to dry. We try to speed it as much as possible by putting it in the sun, or by the stove if inside. The longer it remains wet, the

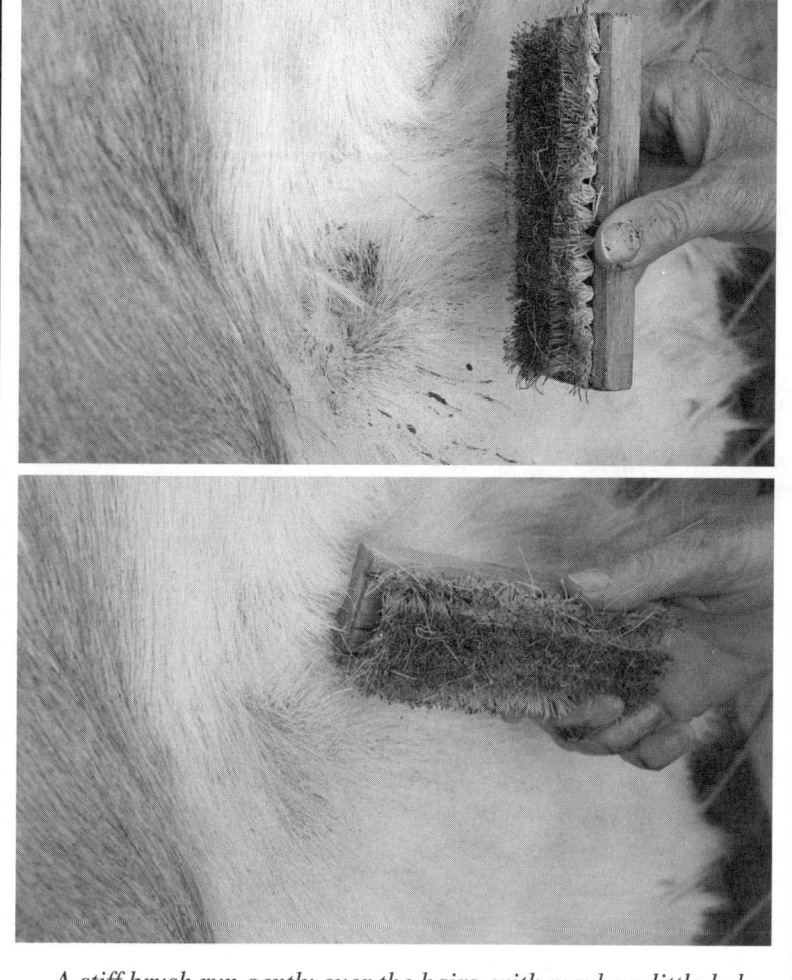

A stiff brush run gently over the hairs, with maybe a little help from your fingers to break up the dried blood, will generally clean the hair sufficiently.

more likely hair slippage ... especially if it had to be soaked.

When dried, sand it lightly. The sanding is not necessary if you've done your job but if you do miss an area and leave a bit of membrane, lets say the size of a half dollar, you'll end with a nickle sized stiff spot. Brain oils won't penetrate thru the membrane - water, being thinner (smaller molecules?) will. The oils will soak in sideways around the membrane a little ... but just so far. Sandpapering lightly will raise up the onion skin-like membrane. If you do find some, just don't grab ahold and pull. This can actually lead to tearing a nice rip in the skin. Sand it away.

This is the time to brush out any dried blood.

BRAINING

Remember, we're after the oils in the brains. That's what will allow the softening. The brains can come from the animal itself or from another. In the past, brains were preserved by mixing with dried moss, grasses or other fibrous material and allowed to dry. The drying needs to take place quickly tho because the brains rot in a hurry ... and what an odor that is! We have used loosely woven moss and also the balled up fibers of hemp and other cordage making plants. You want it loose so that after soaking it in the brains, air will circulate around and thru, hastening the drying. Once dried, they can be stored for extended periods if kept so. Bugs seem to find them so keep them in air tight containers if possible.

Some slaughter houses will allow you to break open the skulls of animals and dig them out. It's nice to have good relations with the local locker and slaughter people. Clean as much bone out of them as you can and freeze them in airtight containers or dry them.

We buy all of our brains from the local super-market by the case - 12 one pound plastic containers for about 15 bucks. Not bad when one will do a buckskin, two a deer robe.

A note here. We have heard of a coupla other tanners getting severe infections by handling uncooked brains with cuts on their hands. Well, we have been handling them for well over a decade - with lotsa cuts - and have had no problems. We do cook our brains but it seems that we always seem to be squishing them in our hands prior. In the instances that we were told about, the tanners were all "wet scrapers". Well, the wet scrape method of removing hair requires that the skin be soaked for a certain period to allow *bacteria* to begin its action. Bacteria! - "Bingo!" We believe that these infections are caused by something other than the brains, just be aware that they could maybe also. Wear-ing of rubber gloves mite be a good idea.

The brains can be rubbed onto the dried skin just as they are, uncooked. There is a certain amount of moisture, besides the oils, in the brain. By rubbing this paste on the skin as it is, rolling it in a ball or covering with plastic or some such to keep it from drying, the oils will be sucked into the skin. Do this with enough brain and over a long enough period of time and you will get the right amount of oils into the thickest part of the skin. Oils have to get thru to the thickest part, all the way to the epidermis on the other side. Remember that when leaving the hair on, brains are being applied only to the flesh side.

What we do is mix about two parts of water to the brain (we use a thinner solution for buckskin). This we kinda squish up with our hands or a spoon and then heat to just about boiling - then let sit until there is no more pink. Grey is the right color (remember, raw works). When we feel that this has steeped enough (whats enough? - anything), we then have to cool it before putting it onto the skin. If it's too hot for *your* skin, it's too hot for the deer's (a good quote I read somewhere recently). If the solution is placed on the skin while too hot, it will ruin it. Just warm to the touch is best. Cold will work but warm seems to have a relaxing effect on the fibers which, in turn, will allow the oils to penetrate more easily. The purpose of the water? Well, water is thinner and will soak in faster and easier than the oils. As it goes, so does the oils. The water seems to draw the oils deeper, faster.

Some people seem to favor wetting the skins with water before applying brains. Something to the effect that the wetted, swelled fibers will allow the oils to penetrate easier. Well, why not just open them with a solution with oils already in it so that you've got a head start? Anyhow, that's what we do.

Lay the stretched skin flat and put bricks or some such under each corner to elevate it. This is to allow air to circulate under, keeping the hair side dry

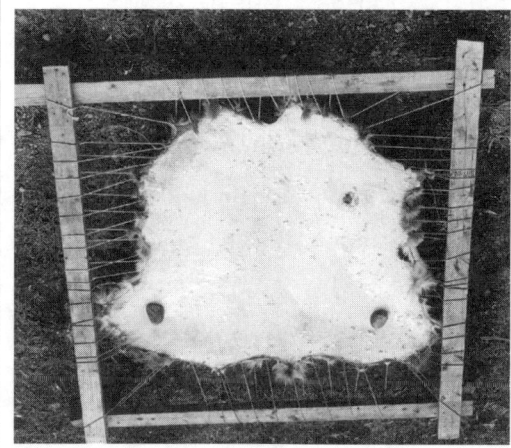

In top photo Geri applies the first coating of the brain solution. Note in photo at left that rocks have been placed on the thicker hams - to keep them lower and thus allow them to absorb better.

while the brain solution soaks in from above. This can be done at one sitting - taking up to several hours - or dragged out over whatever period of time you want. You must allow the solution to soak in completely to the other side - the epidermis. The skin needs to relax itself until it sags. As this happen, the solution will of course flow to the lowest point - the middle. The thickest parts of the skin are the neck, down the backbone area and the hams. To get the solution to spread more evenly, it helps to put weights (rocks) in the heavier ham areas.

#1   To do this at one sitting, let the skin soak up all the liquid and then add more. Repeat until two brains are used (more for bigger, less for smaller).

#2   Apply the solution, let soak in until the skin is completely relaxed, and then dry. Repeat until two brains are used. After the solution has dried it will leave a film of scum on the surface. This needs to be removed before reapplications or it will prohibit the oils from passing thru. Something like membrane. Take any dull, rounded object and scrape. The scraper will work but it covers such a small area. We use tin can tops (smoothed) and here a large spoon. It don't take long but is necessary.

What we did here. We applied one brain solution one afternoon ... let it soak in, dry, scraped and applied the other late another afternoon. After insuring that the second solution had done its job, we covered it

The dried brain solution "scum" needs to be removed between applications.

with a plastic bag (actually two, cut open) and let it sit overnight. This assures good absorbtion. The next morning we uncovered it, placed the frame in an upright position, squeegeed excess moisture out with the same large spoon that we scraped the film with and let it air dry most of the morning. This was done outside as the weather did permit. Otherwise we would have been in near the stove, with windows open for circulation to speed it.

You cannot get too much oil into the skin. You

can easily not get enough. *If there is any "secret" to successful brain tanning, it is getting more than enough oils into the skin*. If you don't get enough in, the product will end up stiff. Getting just enough will work, but you will also - more than is necessary. If you put in extra - the workload drops from this point and the finished product is better.

SEW HOLES

Along about here you'll want to sew up any of the holes that there might be, large and small. Do it while the skin is plenty pliable. A simple whip stitch (that's just around and around) will suffice. Tie it off good as there is gonna be a lot of stress applied

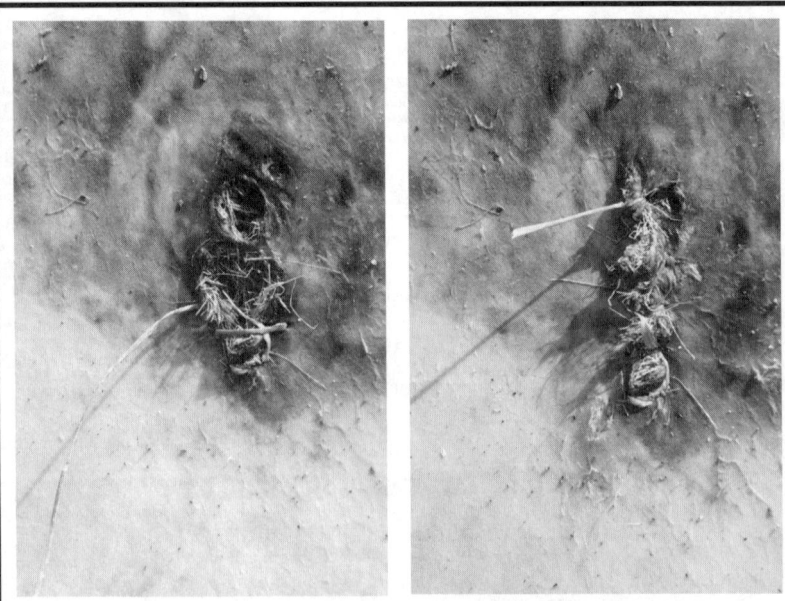

A simple whip stitch with any strong thread will hold the holes together while you finish the robe out.

and there is a good possibility that they mite come undone. Sew even the scores as they will tear while working. Any heavy duty thread will do. Those too close to the edge we don't worry about as we normally just cut the thing from the frame.

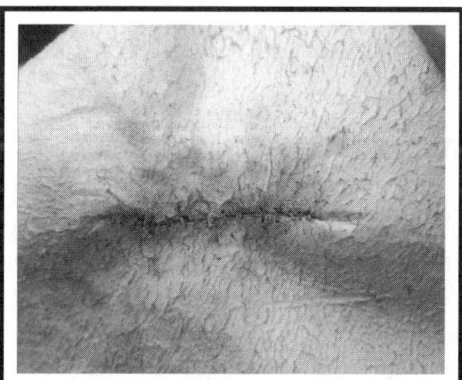

No amount of work will get the edges of these cuts completely soft so we re-sew them after the robe is finished - here using sinew.

FINISHING

Some call it breaking - some stretching. Both are misleading terms as this ain't what is actually happening so we just use the term finishing.

How long to let it air dry varies. You want it to lose a lot of the moisture but it can't get completely dry in any one spot as it will revert back to glue - rawhide - unless the fibers are **manipulated upon themselves**. From now on we (you) need to stay with the project until it is completed. If the skin dries too fast on you ... stiff. We've seen too many paper sacks with hair being called brain tan. That's just what you'll get - or worse - if you let the skin dry without moving those fibers around back and forth on themselves.

In theory, the framed skin can be suspended off the gound in whatever manner and walked/jumped on. In fact we've seen a photograph of Native American women doing just that - but they were holding the edges while throwing small children in the air. The attempts that we have seen trying this method have all been second rate finished products. There is no replacement for good old elbow grease with this. Here's where the staker comes in.

We use a tool that is small enough in diameter to grip easily and with enough weight so that your whole body doesn't have to work as hard. Ideal for me (John) is a one inch diameter iron bar, three to four feet long, with a rounded tip. Nothing needs to be exact. We also use the sway bar off of an old tractor. We do have, and used to use, wooden stakers but found that we had to lean too much into it and wore ourselves out too quickly. The heavier iron allows us to just use our arms. The proper length allows it to be locked into our hips for additional leverage and force when needed.

The idea here is to run this round pointed bar over the entire skin. The skin will dry first at the thinner flanks - so this is where to initially concentrate - but

*Note how Geri is really leaning into the robe with
the bar. Bottom photo really shows the stretch
obtained - here using a pick-ax head.*

you also have to keep the entire skin under control. Two of us generally work at the same time to make it easier ... one working the right side, the other the left - or one working the top while the other concentrates on the bottom. Change positions. One worker is usually stronger than the other and the switching distributes the working more evenly. Overlap. Run the bar to the edge - carefully as the bar wants to run away and there is the chance that you might tear the skin.

You'll see the skin visibly stretch as the bar is pushed in and run across. Keep it moving - cover the entire skin. Every inch. You'll see that by pushing at any point the fibers from many inches away will be moved. Keep the staker moving. Lock it against your body and lean into it. Run it along sewn seams. Up to the very edge of the skin. If you are lucky and have an easy to work skin (normal) and have done your work to this stage correctly, you won't have to fight - just keep it constant. You'll think that the skin is done long before it is. The surface will feel dry - maybe even warm. All the fibers will visibly stretch easily. Good time for a beer break. Come back in an hour or so and it'll have dried to cardboard. Have patience. You'll need a lot of it with this.

The moisture leaves the skin, as it went in, from the flesh side only. The surface will dry - and appear done. But, there is more where that came from. The moisture deep inside against the epidermis is a long time coaxing out. First the surface dries - then the inner moisture slowly comes to the top - not all of it. Once that too is gone, there is still more left behind. How to tell when it is gone? Easy. When you can push the tip of the bar deep into the skin and a wet spot stays when you remove it? Wet. In the later

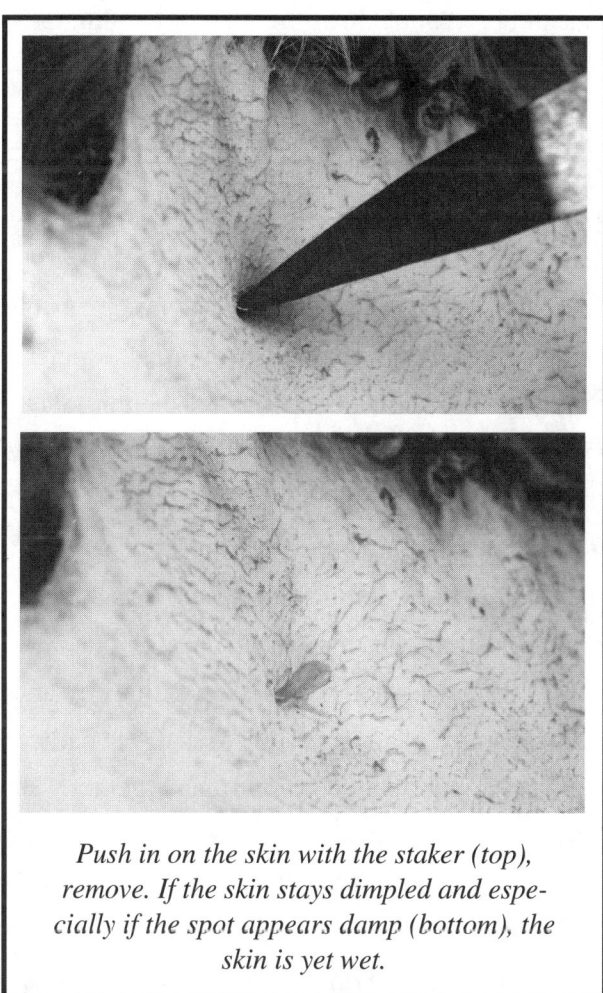

Push in on the skin with the staker (top), remove. If the skin stays dimpled and especially if the spot appears damp (bottom), the skin is yet wet.

stages even this ain't foolproof as there just mite not be too much moisture left. Push the bar and the skin stays dimpled - wet. Push it and the skin seems to bounce back - most, if not all, moisture gone. The for sure sign is when you hear a crackin' sound under the bar. That's just what it is, crackin'. The epidermis is dry - and cracks audibly. You'll hear this first at the thinner flanks. When you hear it overall - you're done.

Towards the end, when there is some crackin' over a goodly portion and the whole thing feels done, you can leave it for short periods. Try 15 minutes or so at first. Do more staking. If it feels real good yet, try a 20 minute break. At the very end when it cracks most all over we leave it for an hour or more at a spell ... but don't ignore it. For that extra fine finished product of a pro you must stay with it. The skin in question here we began working in earnest at noon. We went to bed at ten that night after a coupla one hour breaks. We got up at one to two hour intervals during the night to give it that extra push. It was crackin' all over by one AM.

A little trick that was shared with us by an old time tanner from Nebraska - don't recall his name. For any spots that you feel are stiffer than what they should be ... rewet with alcohol. The tipster said to mix the alcohol with brain oils so that it don't dry too fast - but we have been using it straight in small areas. Dampen the spot you want to work by dabbin' it on with a paper towel or rag and work it - best over a pointed pole, 2x4, or even the edge of a table or chair. The alcohol wets, and so loosens, the fibers - and then evaporates rapidly so you don't have to work as long - or hard.

The final robe should drape over your arm like a blanket, not fold like paper. This ain't a quickie project.

Geri with robe ready to be smoked.

SMOKING - the final step

A kinda quick rehash. We have taken a product that was hard - rawhide. The hide itself, if boiled down, makes one of the strongest glues there is. We inserted oils from brains into this product to coat all of the fibers that make up this skin (like a cottonball, remember?). By keeping the fibers of the drying skin *moving upon themselves* as they dried, they stayed separated. The final product appears like flannel. A good blanket. Now, *if this was to be wetted again, from whatever source, sweat or rain, it would again dry hard unless worked.* Smoking will prevent this.

What we feel is happening is that the oils, creosote or pitch from the smoke, coat and waterproof the individual fibers. The skin itself is not waterproof. Water will flow around all of these separated individual fibers - but the coating of smoke will keep those fibers from actually rewetting - thereby not letting the glue action take effect again.

So how we gonna do this? Well, there are several techniques ... we'll cover a couple here. With buckskin it's a simple matter to sew the skin into a sort of sock and allowing, or forcing, smoke into the hole at the bottom. The smoke then is kinda forced to find it's own way out, most by flowing back out the way it came in - but much is pushed into (or soaked up by) the fibers. When color is showing thru the outside, we then invert the buckskin and smoke the other side for about as long as we did the first side. It's a little tougher to make a sock out of a skin with the hair left in. And robes and pelts are smoked from one direction only.

The way that we did a lot of skins at one time was to hang them in a tipi - kinda like from a clothes line, at the highest points possible. Smoke was then piped in from a stove attended on the outside. In this manner the smoke was not forced into the skin at all, but the skins absorbed smoke from the surrounding air. The first method uses hotter smoke than the second (at least the way that we do it) and is much faster. Absorbing in the tipi took at a minimum eight to twelve hours and then the skins were mostly white in color. To obtain any "brownness", we had to repeat this over two to three days. The direct route takes us *15 to 25 minutes per skin.*

We did the first ever pelts (coyote) that we brain tanned by hanging them in a 4' x 6' smoke house, building a fire in a hole outside and trenching the smoke in (this was in pre-tipi days). It worked. We have heard concerns from various tanners, and others, about the pitch adhering to the hairs and causing stickiness. Well, we haven't had that problem - but then we're not as clean as some others either.

So - method #1 would be to hang them in some enclosure and pipe smoke to the robe or pelt for absorbtion. It does work.

What we more commonly do - because it's faster and easier - is to build a smokey fire in a stove, add several feet of pipe running off horizontally, and turn it up again with an elbow. We then run a thread thru the center of the robe tying it off to a point several feet above the pipe. More threads run from the edge of this, outwards creating a sort of cone - hair up, to the outside. Smoke from the fire is somewhat cooled by running thru the sections of pipe - make them as long or short as you want - and rises into the cone. You will find this works best on a windless day - or even inside of a tipi or other enclosure. Smokey work for sure but its gotta be done. If this has do be done completly exposed to the outdoors, there will most assuredly be some wind. When we do this we will physically hold onto the robe and turn it so that the smoke is more evenly distributed.

How long? Well, it's kinda guesswork, ours coming from experience. Be careful of the tempera-

Smoking of the robe.

ture. Too hot will scorch the product - cook it. No good. Too cool and you'll be there all day (we know several who do this - afraid of the heat - some with good reason). Pay constant attention ... you don't want to ruin all of your labors at this stage. Time? A coupla things to take into account. **Thickness**; size don't make the difference if all is covered with smoke, thickness does. The smoke has to permeate all the way thru. With hair on, this is only from one direction. Thicker skins tanned better - looser fibers - or some such as elk & buffalo which have looser fibers - absorb the smoke more readily. **Temperature**; hanging in the tipi, only cold smoke reaches the skins. The cooler smoke is absorbed more slowly (because the pitch is cooler & thicker?). The hotter smoke is absorbed more readily, don't make it too hot to put your hand in. The skins/robes smoked with cool smoke retain their softness better than those we smoke hot. We assume that this is because of the higher concentration of pitches. When used and washed a few times the product softens to what it was prior to smoking. What we illustrate here is our norm ... pretty warm, almost hot smoke billowing from the stove pipe into the cone ... our average deer takes 30 to 40 minutes.

So that's the process of brain tanning a robe. Just add more of about everything if you set out to work on anything larger than the deer that we illustrated this with. Lets now go thru the steps to do a smaller furbearer.

PELTS

Some of the pelts that we have done are beaver (the hardest), mink, bobcat, possum and coyote. Tried the red fox twice and it was so flimsy that it just fell apart in my hands. About like working wet toilet paper. We'll here do a bobcat. This section will move along at a faster pace because we have already covered terminology and several of the steps in detail. I won't more than touch on skinning because it's a chapter of its own.

We prefer most of our pelts to be "case" skinned - that's like slipping the pelt off as you mite a sock. Cut along the hind legs thru the annus. It's then kinda pulled off. Most animals skinned by trappers will be done this way. They will not leave the skinned out feet on unless requested ... and paid ... to do so. It's time consuming and a pain.

If the animal is opened (split up the belly), it is a bother to work and sometimes you lose some of the edges - especially if you try to lace it to a frame. Best not to.

Beaver are skinned out flat, or open, an exception to the rule of case skinning, and the legs cut off. We sew the legs (& other holes) and lace on a circular frame using a needle and heavy thread. I've also just tacked them out on the side of a shed using long enough nails so that the air will circulate under them.

We cased the cat. We fleshed it at that time with the scraper, on a wire stretcher. A beam would

*(L) On left Geri holds a coyote with fur out and legs cut off -
what you should expect to get from a trapper. In her other
hand she is holding the bobcat that we will be tanning here,
which we skinned leaving the legs and feet on and dried with
fur in. Both are case skinned. (R) Wire and traditional wood
stretchers.*

have worked well here also. It was then allowed to dry -
hair side out - on the stretcher.

We'll begin by going over the entire flesh side
with a fine to medium grit sandpaper. If the fleshing job
was any good at all you won't have much to do. If there
is an excess of meat and membrane left on, sand it until
it is removed. You'll be able to see the membrane the
same as with the deer. Don't pull it. Working around the
face can be interesting. If *properly* skinned, the ears and
lips will be opened up entirely. We usually don't. The

83

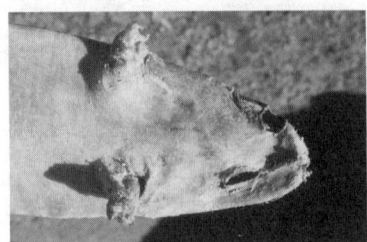

The coyote (L) has been reversed by dampening with wet towel and placed on the wooden stretcher. The cat has had its ears (top) and tail (bottom) skinned correctly. Attention has to be taken to insure that the tail has been opened to the tip to prevent any fats from accumulating there, rotting and slipping the hair.

purpose for this is to separate all the outside from the inside so that tanning solution can get to it. Once dried tho, if kept dried, it will stay preserved so we don't get too concerned about opening it all. Hair might fall out of the ears in time - but then again, maybe not. There is usually meat left on the face. The sharp scraper will come in handy here along with the sandpaper. If broken up, the oils still get through and it will be softened. Depending on the fleshing job, scraping of a goodly area of the skin may be in order.

Use the same brain solution as used on the deer

- maybe even a bit thicker. Remember, you can't get too much on. Cats can be tough in the neck and shoulders.

Apply the brain - let absorb - maybe add some more. The skin absorbs readily. Try not to get too much onto the hair as it becomes a sticky mess (which can be

Scraping and sanding both remove membrane and thin heavier areas in preparation for the brains.

cleaned later tho).

Work the pelt for a lot of the time on a wire stretcher if you have one. It's easy to apply staking motions using many common things. Spoons are good. You can apply a goodly amount of pressure in a small space safely because of the dull, rounded edge. A duller scraper used to do deer works well also. You'll need to keep turning the pelt on the stretcher to get at all the areas.

If you don't have a stretcher the pelt can be worked well enough by hand. Many of the smaller, lighter pelts can be done entirely by hand pulling. Pull and wring, stress it in all directions. Pull it over the corner of tables or chairs. A semi pointed stake driven into the ground works well for this. As with all other

(Top) The brain solution can simply be poured on or applied with a sponge or some such. (L) Liberally apply solution to the feet - also the ears.

brain tanning, keep the fibers of the pelt moving.

I have never gotten a coyote acceptably soft on the first try. Nor a beaver. Don't know the reason. The thing gets kinda ok, but just not brain tanned. More like a paper sack with hair. Brain and work it again. Sometimes even a third time might be necessary. Don't be satisfied with almost. Do it right. Working a coyote dry doesn't take near as long as a deer. A beaver, on the other hand, will try you. The bobcat is somewhere in between. This one took three workings to get the shoulder area accept-

Geri uses a spoon to remove excess brain solution and begin the final finishing process.

ably soft.

Working the tail is fun - ha! Just do the best you can here. It seems to work out. If the legs and feet are left on, you've got extra work cut out. We work these the best we can as we do the main body of the pelt - but if it begins getting away from us (drying too fast), we leave the legs and concentrate all of our efforts on the body

A lot of time can be spent working the pelt over a rope and also a semi-pointed stake driven into the ground. Note our cat checking out the cat (R).

and tail. We go back later and re-wet and finish out the legs. The ideal day for working these is overcast and humid - this slows the drying and allows you to keep in control.

Smoking can be done by hanging in an enclosed

place or approaching as if it were a sewn buckskin ...

As with all brain tanning, smoking is the final step. (L) We allow smoke to flow in the bottom - out the mouth. (Top) The legs and tail should be held in the smoke until you're satisfied with the color.

letting the smoke in the bottom and out the face end.

DUGOUT
CANOE

*T*he spring, summer and fall of 1993 brought heavy flooding throughout the Midwest. The reservoir adjoining our property rose sixty feet. The trash that accompanied this flood included a lot of large logs. One of our local child abo's, a 13 year old girl, came up with the idea of using this mess to our advantage and incorporate one of the larger ones into a dugout canoe.

These local kids had spent the past several years working with some of the basic skills (fire/cordage/traps/basic flintknapping ... and burning bowls). Four of them had spent the previous summer constructing a 9'x9'x17' grass house using nothing but stone tools. They were looking for a challenge.

What they envisioned was scouring the lake shore for a large enough log and burning it to length and shape. They know the rules that apply here - any project that we work on like this is to be done primitively, using stone tools. I tried to talk them out of it.

"You know," says I, "that we gotta do this the right way. With stone."

"Yeah".

"You know this ain't gonna be easy. Lotsa work."

"Yeah."

I went on to explain that finding the "right" log is about out of the question. Trees that die and dry out uncontrolled crack, I explained. Cracked canoes ain't good. I also explained that in my mind, burning wasn't the best way to do this. "Lotsa chopping", I said.

"Yeah".

So it was born.

I placed a number of phone calls to friends and acquaintances around the country who might be able to give me information on this project. The consensus was that this project had not been attempted in recent times using nothing but primitive methods. In fact, building a dugout using modern tools wasn't a real common thing. One contact, Scott Silsby of Virginia, sent me two ground stone adze heads for helpers.

I hollowed out a two foot section of a green cottonwood limb into some semblance of what we might be after. It seemed to work OK.

I decided to use cottonwood as I had heard and

Our tool chest ... kinda on the small side but a good assortment.

read of this being used traditionally. Also it was readily available. Large diameter, straight and limb free trunks are common hereabouts.

The tools that we had to work with were not really axes. What I had in my store were more along the line of hatchets. Of course, the majority of the kids that were to be in on this project were on the small side so it kinda worked out.

15 year old Ken Neilson ready to begin, holding what at the beginning were our two best axes.

I had spent some days looking around the area for the "right" tree - and found one about eight miles from here that the landowner said we could have. This particular tree gave us about 20 feet of clean trunk before the first limb was encountered. It grew alongside a small creek at the base of about a 30 foot cliff. Getting it out might be a problem, but we'll cross that when we get to it.

27 June 1994

As with most major endeavors, the first step is the hardest. With one helper, strapping 15 year old Ken Neilson, I went to work. Using a coupla of my better axes/hatchets and backed up with a coupla adzes, we began.

"Damn. What did I get into here."

Chop, chop, chop, all day long ...
chop chop, chop, I sing this song ...

We began chopping the undercut - the direction we wanted the tree to fall - at a reasonably comfortable height. And we chopped. And chopped.

"Ooooh! This is big!"

94

I mean, it really is impressive just what can be done with stone tools. I'm always amazed at the efficiency of stone. But what we were removing with these small tools compared to what there was to be removed seemed minuscule. Wow!

Well, we did. Ken and I chopped for six hours that first day. And by the end of the day, we saw that we had done something. To move a mountain, you've gotta get that first shovel full. We were on our way. This first day we had cut a goodly section out from the side that we wanted the tree to fall (undercut), up the

(L) Daisy Behrens, 13 chops while brother Jason, 11 rests. (R) Jeremie Behrens, 15, on left, Jason, Jared Henry, 13, Ivan Anderson, 11 and Daisy (at top) rest on fallen tree.

cliff.

Day two, two days later, additional help showed. Ken didn't make it but five others did. By the end of the day we had enlarged the undercut and gotten most of the upper (felling) cut out on the opposite side. A good wind would drop it. The third day the full crew showed and in two hours it was down. Actually it was more of a leaning - up the cliff where we needed it to be. To insure that it fell this direction I had run a rope from the tree to the back of my pickup.

I used a chain saw to cut the small end off. This procedure was tricky even with the saw ... it would have been impossibly dangerous using axes. I had decided that this would be done at the beginning. The challenge here was in the felling. I'd have used the saw if it had fallen flat on the ground. An army tank retriever was used to get it up the cliff and onto a trailer which we used to haul it to our place.

Fourteen hours over two days to fell the tree. For six of the hours there were only two of us. The rest of the time there were six. Not all six were able to work at one time so we worked in shifts. No matter how you count the hours, we were happy that we did as well as we did - considering that half of the kids had no experience in working with stone tools and all of the tools were small sized ... as were most of the kids.

Several parents and neighboring farmers and ranchers stopped by. Lots of head scratching and advice as to the efficiency of the chain saw was offered.

Hauling the trailer w/log to our place, off loading and rolling it to where we wanted to work it took only a coupla hours.

Ivan (lower L), Ken and I with log loaded for trip home.

I had concerns about it drying out on us. Any wood that dries too fast will split. This log, cottonwood, was heavy with its own *natural* moisture (water). When we put up bow staves (most of my past experience of working with wood) I paint the ends of the logs immediately to keep water from leaving from the ends, where it will leave first. Some woods will begin developing cracks (checks) immediately after cutting. Elmer's type glues work well for this purpose and this we painted on the ends. Keeping it moistened will slow down the drying. Figuring that this project would take some time, we put the log under some cedars to keep it in shade,

97

placed it on other, smaller logs to keep it off the ground, placed straw underneath and kept the whole affair wetted down at all times. When we were not actually working on it, it was covered with a tarp.

Ivan sits on log in front of grass house built the previous summer. Here it will be converted into a beam.

As bark is the tree's raincoat, I wanted to leave it on as much of the log as was possible while we worked it. Knowing no difference, having no blueprints besides the idea of something that would float once hollowed out, I planned to square the log so that we would have a flat bottom, the most stable shape I could think of. I've canoed (modern) before and know just how unstable something like this could turn out.

"*Tues., 5 July - Ken, Ivan, Reo and I chopped 7 1/2 hours total flattening top* (actually a side). *Slow going getting used to tools*" reads my notes. We experimented. Bark was removed in sheets from 18 to 24" at a time, working, in teams, from both ends of the log. Once the bark was off from a section, we then used adzes and axes to flatten the surface. I ran a cord (hand made) along both sides from end to end to serve as a guide. We cut a cross groove (score) in the log down to the cord with axes and used axes and adzes to remove

Handmade cordage in place as used for guideline in flattening the log.

the wood. The next day we were joined by another (Evan) and put in another 7 1/2 hours. They slept here that night (Wed., 6 July) and put in another 5 1/2 hours Thursday. They finished flattening the first side this day. *They* wanted off over the weekend.

I wasn't real exact on my time keeping. When you have a boy to help, you get the help of one boy. When there are four, there is a lot of horse play. In fact I about had to ask one of the guys not to return but after talking it over he decided that he wanted to stick with the project. So when I record four boys plus myself working for x number of hours, I can't multiply that number by four. Also, there was a lot of down time - time where I was kept occupied with the repair of tools - mostly handles and re-sharpening. And breaks. There were a lot of breaks. We have a pond not far from the place and much time was spent there. The days were hot, approaching 100°. I tried not to include pond time. So I got a bit sloppy with my timecards - but I tried.

Jeremy, Evan Risdon (15) and Reo Schultz (13) work on flattening another side.

They had the weekend off. But I saw the enormity of what lay before us. I took Friday off but was back at it Sat. and Sun. I've got a terribly sore back from an old military injury so my days tend to be shortened. I put in four hours each day working on flattening the bottom, which was, of course, now on the top. Monday three of the boys showed and we got this second side finished. *"Ivan stayed late (overnite) to help."* ... a positive sign of things to come.

It went on this way for several more days. Some days just me - other days there were seven. From four to seven hours a day. At times I repaired tools in the afternoon while the kids occupied themselves. Other times this was done in the evening. Just one person to help with the upkeep of tools would have been a major contribution. I didn't dare to let the kids work on the canoe unsupervised ... one mistake could have been disastrous.

The final piece to remove to make the log a beam.

We began this project on 27 June. We got the fourth side flattened on 15 July. 15 total working days so far, three of them in chopping the tree down and one in moving it.

Why, one might ask, square the log? Well, I had very limited information and photographs to refer to when I began this project. A couple of the larger origi-

(Top) Evan and Jeremy do some "finishing" work while Jason (L), Daisy, Evan, Jeremy and Bob Grant, 16, roll the beam over (bottom).

nal canoes that I saw pictured appeared to be squared - so be it. If I were to do it again, would I square it? probably not. Why? Because I think that I would retain more strength by keeping the sides, at least, in one growth ring - and this would most likely allow me to stretch it further (more on this later) to widen the canoe

- plus I would retain width by not flattening the sides - at the loss of some depth. If the log was large enough I could still work the bottom flat. Gotta make trade-offs. I wanted this canoe large enough to float as many of these kids as possible.

The use of a chain saw would make the squaring/shaping of this log less than a one day project. With stone it took us eleven.

I have read that the use of stone here in America for wood working was common - except for the stone ax which was used only for girdling trees. *Poppycock*!

Girdling the tree will cut off the life support to the tree, there-by killing it ... slowly, over a period of time. Then, I have seen in print and heard, it is a simple matter to burn the tree down. I wonder just how much control one has over the fire that is trying to burn *up* this tree. I have a feeling that it would be a bear to keep under control. But, it might be so.

If a small group of completely inexperienced youngsters working with small hatchet sized tools can chop down a 30" diameter tree - that's BIG folks - in fourteen hours, think of what five or six experienced, brawny men could do with real man sized axes. I think no more than half a day, if that.

We went from a tree, to a log, to a beam. We also ran out of time. Geri and I had an appointment on the Blackfeet Indian Reservation in Montana the first week of August. We also had to make a stop in NW

Montana to peel tipi poles cut for us by friends on the way - since we would be living in our tipi while with the Blackfeet. And it's most of a three day drive from here (NW, E Kansas - huh?) to there. We had to hit the road. So Geri and I chained the beam to the back of the pickup, dragged it to a pond in the neighboring pasture and submerged it.

Bow staves can be cured by submerging them - they will lose their moisture while soaking - I don't pretend to understand it, only it's true. Old time dugouts from thousands of years back are found on a regular basis in pretty good shape - submerged. We figured that what worked for them would work for us. We drove two pairs of cross sticks in deep enough water to cover the canoe. Tying the sticks tightly as we could while sitting on the ends, keeping the beam submerged, worked better than I could have hoped. As I took a run thru the pasture the next day I found I needed to drive the sticks deeper - one end had risen. I redid it and it now held.

My notes pick up again on *Thurs., 25 Aug. Back to it - working ends to shape - began on large end. Like chopping tree down again.* ... Now that the log had become a beam, both ends needed to be shaped. The large end was what we had chopped. The other was an *embarrassing* saw cut. The thing was heavy! I pushed the large end up on the shore as far as I could, prying from behind with a pole and began to chop, making

104

sure that I had the bottom up (there is a slight curl to the beam which I feel will add to the canoe's shape pointing both ends upwards).

The temp was running at & over 100° so school was called off during the heat of the afternoon. About the smallest (in size) helper I had this season, 13 year old Ivan Anderson, showed up to work with me three of the afternoons. We could force the ends of beam only just so far out of the water ... you can't chop underwater ... at least we couldn't. Our final working day of 1994 was on 28 August - both ends nearly, but not quite, done. We then submerged it and just never got back to it again until the next summer.

Ivan and I put in the final day of work for 1995 by working on the ends.

1995 - from Beam to Canoe

Monday, 5 June 1995 Jason, Bob, Ivan and I surfaced canoe 1st time this season - water deep - had to search for log - was to chin when standing (on log) - *had to dive to untie it. Shaped small end but couldn't get too far up because ground was real soaked* (to pull further w/pickup) - *buried in shallow water - too much horse play (from two of the kids).*

Time off for a teaching trip to Colorado.

Ivan rides the beam to the surface for another day of work.

Tues. June 27 - Began to make a <u>canoe</u>. Started small end for about six feet - only two hours - Ivan & me.

Now we have a canoe! We got dug in for only two inches or so, but we were <u>in</u>. Alright!

Axes were used to cut the outside boundaries of what we wanted to remove, leaving initially about 12 inches at either end and two inches at the sides ... this

106

was done for right at six feet on the large end. It was easiest for us to sit on the canoe and chop a sort of dotted line about two inches in from the initial perimeter groove, just kinda stripping away the slivers of wood (cottonwood is stringy). It went along pretty fast. Sitting as we did, our backs were able to be in a mostly upright position letting our arms take the brunt of the workload.

Speaking of the arms taking the *brunt* of the load ... last season's chopping had about made my right shoulder and elbow quit. I got a pretty good swelling of the joint at the collarbone and the neckline (I never knew of such a joint). Lotsa pain. It ain't right yet. All of the constant pounding must not be real good for the body.

Now let me talk Ivan for a minute. Ivan Anderson. Thirteen. Lives about 5 miles down the road from us. 4'10", 85 pounds - of rompin', stompin' abo. He was the one helper this season who showed up just like clockwork. Ivan and I made the beam into a canoe. He has wonderfully supportive parents who encourage their children to follow *their own* interests ... it shows in the achievements of his brother and sister also. It's just that Ivan loves the outdoors. The rougher and more primitive, the better. He runs most every morning with Geri and I before school ... anywhere from two to five miles a lick. Fall and winter nights he spends chasing after coon dogs. You'll see more of Ivan in later chapters of

107

this book.

On with the tale. We hit it most days. Maybe four on, two off, six on, and so on (ha!). Anywhere from two hours to seven and a half, probably averaging four or so a day. And when I write *two* people *working*, that's what I mean. Ivan was like a mad dog chawing

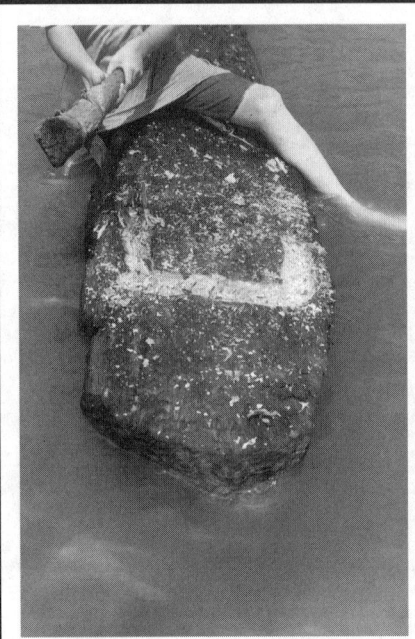

We began by cutting an outline and removing the insides (L), but found it more expedient to chop a line down the middle and removing wood outwards (R).

away at that log. Foot by foot, inch by inch, we pulled those slivers of wood out and the hollow kept getting deeper. We changed our method from outlining the perimeter to cutting a channel down the middle and then chopping that dotted line to either side. The growth

rings separated easily and the wood stripped away
pretty cleanly. Just a lot of repetition day after day. One
day we were about four inches deep from end to end
and Ivan & I both floated in it. We needed paddles.

*Ivan cuts down 5" tree, flattens it, shapes it and
ends with a rough paddle.*

The afternoon temperature was right at 107° - so we quit the pond, picked up our stone axes and headed into the timber to cut a coupla cedars for at least temporary paddles. We found and chopped down two fairly straight trees, cutting them to about 5 1/2 feet lengths. Ivan commented that this "seemed awfully easy after working on the canoe". We cut them to length at about 5 1/2 feet so that they might also be used in poling. The width of the tree determined the width of the paddle and in the timber, contrary to cutting most trees, these were smaller than at first appeared. Ivan's was right at 5" wide, mine closer to 6".

We began by flattening the piece the entire length, removing from two sides to retain the width of the log, then cutting in from the sides at a point above the paddle to the tip - where we left a slight knob. We figured rightly that the finished product would be warped but didn't care as that didn't matter for our purpose. We took them to the pond and kept them submerged with the canoe to help stabilize the wood while it was drying. They work. Though smaller than what we will want for the finished canoe, they work remarkably well to move us around the pond. We have maybe three hours total per paddle. Making a wider one won't take too much longer.

Several old knots appeared while we worked thru the cottonwood - spots where limbs had fallen off and had been grown over. These proved to be somewhat of a pain as they slowed progress but we just kept pecking away following the growth pattern around them and suddenly they disappeared.

Knots were a pain and slowed us but by carefully chopping around them they eventually dissappeared.

The daily temperature during July ran around 100° but working in the pond kept us comfortable. We drank lots of water & swam to find the cooler spots when we needed the break. When we passed the center mark of the log I figured that things would be easier - and in some ways they were. The growth rings at this point began to angle upwards from center and kinda made it easier to expose more of the ring surface and thereby remove more material at a lick. The center ring in particular just kinda popped out. But the deeper that

The deeper we dug, the harder it was to find a comfortable working position.

*When we reached this depth, somewhat past center, the
bending hurt too much to fight at this location so we
moved the canoe to home where we at least didn't have to
fight the sucking mud.*

we continued, the more that we had to bend our backs. Ivan began to complain about the soreness (something he hadn't done before) and my back screamed. The pond we were at sank us above our ankles as we moved about sucking our boots off (we wore as protection from leeches) ... changing positions was a pain - really. The awkward positions that the deeper cut canoe forced us to work in was something. Sometimes we kneeled in the mud - we tried moving to deeper water but without the canoe held in position it would swing away from us. In the canoe to chop with axes, in the pond or mud using the adze. Nothing was seeming to work. I decided to move it home.

This decision was not made without some thought. My main concern as we went along was that it would dry too quickly, developing cracks. I contacted the Forestry department at Kansas State University. "Why cottonwood", he said. "Its going to crack. Dry it slowly."

I called the National Geographic Society Research Department. "You know more about this than we do", was the response. "Dry it slowly."

I called the National Forests Products Laboratory. "Going to crack. Dry it slowly." They did advise not to use a sealant (my idea) but to bury the finished canoe in a pile of chippings or straw to slow down the drying.

I called a fellow in Maryland by the name of Tony Breda who has made several dugouts using steel and fire over the years. He said that "if it cracks, just seal it up".

I don't want it to crack!

A year or so prior I had made a table for the house out of green eastern red cedar. After assembling all components I sealed it completely with various varnishes, linseed oil and water seals ... whatever I had on hand at the time. It audibly cracked (a tiny *visible* crack on the under side) once a coupla months later. Geri sealed it again with linseed oil and it hasn't cracked again. It has lost weight and shrunk quite noticeably around pegs that hold it together.

I worry now about this. I'm dealing with a much wetter wood ... and I have a lot more time and effort involved. Seems as if I've got to make the call.

Once I remove it from the water, I gotta do something. **Fast**. As long as it remained submerged I didn't concern myself with this as all was stable. But we don't live on the water and I wouldn't feel secure about leaving it anywhere except in my own back-yard. Once I get it home it's gonna dry.

Hmmmmmmm.

There is less likelihood of checking and warpage if the entire product is of equal dimensions

... like maybe a two inch thickness overall. I'm just not gonna make that. I want my ends somewhat thicker for more strength (maybe I'm wrong, my call). And I don't really want to trust a two inch thickness on the twenty foot long bottom. Well, while I continue to ponder the situation, we get it home.

Geri, Ivan and I head to the pond with a hay trailer behind our four wheel drive and back the flat

Ivan and I take one last ride (top) before loading the dugout onto the trailer for the trip home (bottom). Note how high the canoe floats at this stage - after finishing it's about 5 inches higher and very un-stable for two persons.

bed trailer as deep in the pond as we dare. Now I don't have any idea just how much this thing weighed at this point - just that it was *heavy*. We ran the small end of the canoe to the trailer and tied a rope around it. Need be careful here as too much stress on the open sides could collapse it. We hook a "come along" winch to the bumper of the truck and use nylon rope in between. Geri & I are at either side of the small end and are having a time getting it 12 inches or so *up* to the trailer ... Ivan works the come along. Somehow, someway, the end of the canoe sits on the end of the trailer. Ivan sucks up the come along until we're afraid that the rope will break and then Geri and I do a three count and *oomph* the canoe forward a coupla inches. Again. And again. After probably not much more than an hour, it rests comfortably on the trailer. After tying it down, Geri and Ivan sit back there to stabilize it as I drive carefully home. Doesn't seem like it was just over a year ago that we unceremoniously dragged the beam the other direction on the same path.

Once at our place we park the trailer/canoe in the shade of some large cedars. Gotta keep it from drying out, cracks you know.

You, the reader, may feel that I'm kinda overstressing this drying/cracking business ... but this is a very real concern of mine. I've explained the how's and whys of this earlier on. As I sit and write this, early January of 1996, it's still on my mind. When we brought the canoe here from the pond I can only estimate its weight - maybe 700 lbs. I would guess it now would run about 300#. I hope that it will end up about 250# - so, in my estimation, it's probably past any real worry stage (*and it ain't cracked!*). But at the time that I'm writing *about*, I've got a waterlogged/soaked canoe. If the moisture was to leave uncontrolled, I've got cracks. If the moisture stays in too long, I've got another worry ... rot. Kinda between a rock and a hard spot. Try to place yourself in my mindset as we venture here.

The wood is much easier to remove when it is wet. Even while working at the pond, the surface would dry out and we would rewet it to make the chopping easier. When wet, the blades cut in like sharp tools should. When the stringy cottonwood would dry out some, the tools seemed to crush more than cut. So we wanted to keep the canoe wet, yet get it dried as soon as possible. Remember, I've got no one to turn to for suggestions. If the National Geographic Society and National Forests Products Laboratory can't help me, well, I guess I'm on my own. So I'm wingin' it. The only solution is to work *fast* to finish the wood removal stage and get the thing drying ... *slowly*.

So we went at it. The canoe was now sitting on the trailer at a height of about three feet. We would climb aboard, sit astride the canoe and chop with the ax. Or stand in it and work with the adze. Whatever position was most comfortable on us ... either tool worked. We turned it over and worked the ends again from the ground or standing on a stump, whichever fit best. Remember that we took this out of the pond mostly because of the discomfort of working positions. Things now were a little better.

We were another twelve days (several of them nonworking) before I considered we were done. We had gotten a load of Rhyolite (a tough, flint type rock) in from "Rocky" Culbertson of NC to whom I had mentioned that I was short of large pieces of good raw tool material. I made up several blades and hafted them on very short handles which made for easier working inside, not only the bottom but also the sides. Ivan also wanted to work at something else for a change so he tanned up a deer skin while I worked tools. We had put a pretty good coating of water seal on the canoe & relished the non-stress while I worked things out in my mind. We took off a lot of material at both ends ending up with about eight inches thinness at either. The bottom averaged out at four inches and the sides at about two and a half. A good load of granite rock was gathered for the next step.

Fri., 18 Aug. - Hot rocked - Really "hot". We built a pyre of cedar and hedge wood layered with the granite and torched it. We filled the canoe about two

119

thirds full of water. We was gonna boil.

Lots of amazing bending tricks can be done to wood that is heated. More so if steam/wet heated. The heat (alone, or with the addition of moisture) will loosen the fibers of the wood allowing it to be stressed far beyond normal without deformation - and it will retain this shape. We had heard of this being done both historically and prehistorically with canoes and we elected to do it. The canoe at the large end

Ivan building the rock pyre.

leaked where the center growth ring was rotted - this we stuffed with hemp fibers which swelled and slowed it to a drip. When the fire had burned down enough that we could get somewhat near it, we went to work.

Using sticks, we rolled rocks from the coals and onto a cedar limb that we had broken only partway through and then bent back on itself & tied with a strip of rawhide giving us two sticks side by side which we used as a rock carrier. The rocks were so hot that they made the bark burst into flames tho the sticks themselves never did burn through. The water heated - fast. It took us maybe 40 minutes to get all the rocks into the water filled canoe (we used shovels at the last) and by the time that we were finished it was boiling the entire length. Hot!

Here Ivan places hot rocks into the water filled canoe - this, the 2nd heating, gained us an extra 5 inches in spots.

Once we had all of the rocks in the canoe we began to wedge in lengths of wood about 5-6" diameter cut at a bevel forcing the sides out. At first it felt as if we were forcing the wood, though it did give willingly - but by the time that we had placed five or so down the length, the first wedges were loose and needed to be replaced. The sides spread smoothly and evenly. For most of the length we gained right at three inches. Once we felt we had done what good we could do, we left all in place until the next day when I off loaded the rocks and bucketed out the water. I left the wedges in for now.

Using a pile of wooden blocks and saw horses as steps, we levered the canoe to the ground and placed a log under either end to keep it from direct contact with the earth. The canoe was oiled again, this time with boiled linseed oil. I checked it every day looking for any signs of cracking and after about two weeks I noticed that a crack was developing at the bottom, on the inside. The log/canoe was shrinking and the wedges were preventing the top from follow- ing the bottom - and the side was trying to separate. I immediately pounded out the wedges ... there seems to be no ill effects from the crack that was apparently just beginning. Inspections once or twice a day during this period were important. It was losing moisture and other than this episode, no cracks.

Since bringing the canoe from the pond we had kept it covered with wetted old wool army blan- kets and a tarp. Once placing it on the ground we turned it upside down, put short lengths of sticks across the top, a long cedar pole on top of that. At either end we let the wool blankets drape down somewhat protecting the more vulnerable to cracking ends. (I say more vulnerable to cracking because here the growth rings are more or less intact - the inner ones drying (& shrinking) at a different rate that the outer. The blankets (& over them the tarp) are placed over this "kinda sheathing" created by firewood & poles so that there is an air space to allow circulation. I want it to dry and if the protecting blankets and tarp are in direct contact with the canoe, it won't as well.

At about this time I tackled the "split ends" ... the rotten core. The large end was the worst and I had dug out as much of the rotted core as I could earlier. Several cracks radiated out from this, probably caused as the tree fell. I pounded a hard piece of wood into these cracks to enlarge them so as to make it easier to fill. A short length of cedar just slightly larger in diameter than the rotted center hole was worked to a tapering point ... about eight inches long.

I (I hate to say this) *bought* a container of roofing cement - tar - and used this as a sealant. Pine pitch was probably used where it existed as well as was tar (asphaltum) in days gone by. I was satisfied with our "primitiveness" to date and for the third major time gave in to the modern world (#1 sawing the small end & #2 using waterseals). I took this modern day asphaltum, mixed it with hemp fibers to

123

(Top L) Hole in large end,
Fibers, plug and maul (L)
and the
plugged hole (top R).

help hold it together and crammed it into the cracks and the center hole. After a liberal coating of tar, the cedar peg was then pounded into the center until I saw that the perimeter was spreading - then another coupla light taps for good measure. I didn't want to overdo this as the tree was still shrinking and if forced into the end too tightly it may lead to further cracking.

So, there it is. 66 total days worked during two summers. 278.5 one man hours - 92 in 1994 and 186.5 in 1995. Results: one twenty foot long dugout canoe done in just about its entirety with primitive methods.

When we took it from the pond it floated three

Handling the dugout can be a chore even for the best of groups. Here Daisy (shoulder on L, to R), Reo, Derick Hargrave, Ken, Bob and Jason struggle with the behemoth.

of us (350#) with room to spare. It had a list to one side which I am waiting for it to dry completely before removing wood from the *outside bottom of the high side* - buoyancy - to correct. It was stable enough that Ivan and I could paddle standing. Ivan alone (85#) was not able to make the canoe take on water no matter how he tried. Since we took it to dry dock, we have removed about another three to four inches from the floor (inside) and eight inches or so from each end - which is *weight removed* and *buoyancy gained*. The canoe has also lost a lot of its weight through drying ... more buoyancy.

What is the result of this? It may lose some of its stability but will ride higher - carry more people. If we desire more stability for fewer people we'll simply

*The almost finished product as it stands today (above) and the
entire gang (minus 1) gathered for a group photo.
From (L); Evan Risdon, Reo Schultz, Derick Hargrave,
Ken Neilson, Bob Grant, Daisy, Jason &
Jeremy Behrens and Ivan Anderson.
Missing is Jared Henry,*

add rocks as ballast. We do know that we have a canoe that works and have only improved on it since bringing it here. We'll have to wait until warmer weather to give it the final try and finishing touches.

Finishing touches? Yep. (1) The three inches we gained in width by hot rocking, we lost again to shrinkage - so we'll do it again and hope it'll stretch some more. (2) A final coating of some sort of permanent protection from any of the elements needs be applied (prehistorically the entire canoe was scorched with fire to seal and protect it). And (3), as mentioned above, we need to remove wood from the proper places to make for level floating.

Then ... we're gonna spend some time on the river.

SOME CONCLUSIONS.

Ax type tools did more work than adzes.

Flaked flint tools performed better than ground ones and required much less time to make.

I feel that chopping out a dugout is more time efficient than burning with much less chance of cracking. I'm convinced that 5 to six experienced adults with another one or two to keep up maintenance on the tools could repeat this feat in less than three weeks, most likely less than two.

ADDENDUM

The prior was written during the winter of

1995/'96 ... it is now Sept. '96. This past summer found us with not as much time to spend on the canoe as we had hoped. We reheated with water and hot rocks and got the sides to spread another five inches in spots. When we took it to the water we found that the buoyancy gained was kind've a bother. It now floats *very* high ... I guess that's what I was after tho. Either Ivan or I could kinda handle the thing ourselves - putting the two of us in at the same time and we fought for balance. With Geri added we lost all control at all. Adding more people or ballast in the form of rocks would help tremendously. The thing just floats high.

The list remains ... of course. After we got it back to dry dock we removed a layer of wood from the *outside of the high side.* We haven't got it back into the water again yet. Building the right trailer is a next project for this. It now rides on a 4 wheel trailer and if you have any experience with these, you'll know that they are not the best to be packing a 250 pound canoe around on - so there is a real inconvenience in moving it to water.

Stone tool Dugout canoe project
- 278.5 hours - 66 days - two summers
averages 4.5 hours per day -

Roster of workers.

Name	Age	Hours worked
John McPherson	50-----------	278.5 --- total hours -
Ivan Anderson	13 -----------	174.25
Evan Risdon	14------------	40.5
Reo Schultz	13------------	39
Ken Neilson	16------------	29.5
Jason Behrens	13------------	25.5
Jeremy Behrens	16------------	23.5
Daisy Behrens	14------------	23.5
Bob Grant	16------------	17
Derick Hargrave	13------------	12
Jared Henry	15------------	8

- 671.25 - totaled hours -
66 days -two summers -

• Summer 1994 - Year one •

14 hours -------3 days to chop tree down.
61.5 hours -----12 days to square into beam
16.5 hours -----4 days shaping ends
92 hours   19 days total 1994

• Summer 1995 - Year two •

133.25 hours ---35 days digging out at pond
53.25 hours ----12 days at the house (drydock) ... deepening,
squaring, shaping ... sealing rotted center and
cracks ... filling with water, hot rock boiling and
widening.
Then was covered to protect from moisture
and promote slow drying - sealed with repeated
coatings of linseed oil/mineral spirit mixture
to further slow drying.
186.5 hours - 47 days total 1995

*(Records were not kept for 1996. Approx. 25 hours put
in hot rock widening, launching once and trimming list.)*

Since having completed what you have just read, we have been contacted by Jack McKee, then of Alaska, now of Idaho, who has been a boat builder (including many dugouts) for many, many years and also, like ourselves, a student of primitive lifestyles. He had noted in a write-up on us somewheres that we had been working on this project and so he took the opportunity to write us.

He writes books, not letters. We have had several packets from him running 30 to 50 pages of hand written experience and lore. He's literally a warehouse of knowledge and he has given us permission to pass some of this on to you. I highlighted what I perceived as pertinent when I initially read thru these "books" of his and here list some of what I feel might directly pertain to this chapter.

• He uses the word "naturalistic" thru-out in place of "primitive" ... fitting. (Note chapter 5-I.)
• A straight sided boat loads down much faster than one with flair sides. (Ours was built straight and then flaired somewhat by hot rocking.)
• The addition of one part urine to two parts water (actually the ammonia) will soften the wood more while hot rocking to spread sides.
• Use battens at the sides to achieve more even spreading.
• While hewing a canoe to be spread, the sides should be left higher towards the middle so that they will be equal when spread apart.
• All boats can be divided into thirds. 1/3rd for each end and 1/3rd for the middle.
• When spreading, spread from the middle out.
• "Stabilty in a boat is in its LENGTH ... NOT WIDTH!! Remember this always!!"

- "Two boats of of the same material and same weight racing - the one with the longest waterline will win --- it is faster! Even with the exact same amount of energy used to propel both boats."
- "The safest of all waterline lengths the world over, regardless of the water, including oceans, is 25 feet!"
- " ... if you want to learn the intellectual degree of a people -- look at their weapons and boats and how they construct housing."
- Fire will temper the ends of logs to help prevent splitting.
- To test if a tree is solid enough for your purpose, auger a hole. It can be plugged using a limb from the same tree.
- When downing a large tree, chop a groove above and below - wedge out the middle portion.
- Many NW coast canoes were made from rot hollowed trees. End caps were made, holes drilled in hull and cap and then sewn together with cedar root and caulked.
- Our design - "a very universal design for rivers".
- "All native vessels had *flex* in a sea way and they seldom, if ever, broke up. ... Modern vessels all fight the waves."
- He mentioned in his first letter that it is best to always "overbuild" tools ... and in his most recent went on to elaborate that maybe that wasn't quite the right way to phrase it. "When we speak of stone tools, we must match the tool to the one who uses it most!" Build tools for the individual and use them for tasks that don't abuse them by overuse. "Reduce those shocks that cause sore muscles and joints and ligament damage over periods of long use!" ... which I am now aware of

... by making tools that flex. "The abilty to absorb shock to the body limbs is perhaps as much a consideration as any other part of the tool!"

•

Hey ... we don't know Jack McKee and can't verify his past or experience ... but ... what he has shared with us over the past months we have found to be truths. One doesn't come up with the thoughts and ideas that he has expressed from an easy chair. He's done it. He needs to put in print form the stuff that he has shared with us - here you get only a glimpse. We thank him for allowing us to share some of it.

These next two pages have been left blank so that we can more easily add photo's and information in later printings of the canoe finally making its premier voyage.

Chapter
5

Odds
'n Ends

*I*ncluded here are several ideas,
tips, & what have ya's.
Enjoy.

5 - A
FLINTKNAPPING

C hapter nine of our last book gives a good introduction to flintknapping - the predictable removing of flakes from stone. I won't go into that introduction any more here except to stress a coupla of what we feel are the most important aspects for the basic understanding of flintknapping.

Rule #1. Flint type rocks break conchoidally (you needn't remember the word), meaning that <u>the angle of the energy from the striking force changes direction upon contact</u> - **into a cone** (as when a small stone or BB strikes a window). This is the number one rule of flintknapping and once this sinks in, a light will go on in your head. *All other rules stem from this*.

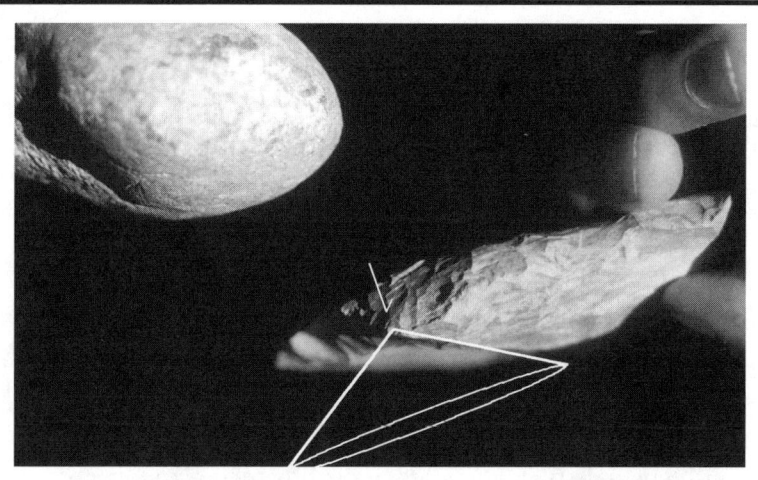

This photo illustrates all three of the primary rules of flint-knapping. The cone (#1) shoots the energy at an angle to the blow along a ridge (#2) off a solid striking surface (#3).

Rule #2. You cannot remove predictably more than one half of a cone in flintknapping.

Rule #3. You need a solid striking surface (referred to as a platform), ideally just somewhat less than 90° from where the flake is to be removed (90° is right at the too much, 45° close to the too little).

These rules are gone into in more depth in the above referred chapter. Here I just want to add some of what we have determined to be pretty important tips (rules) to advance one beyond the simple removal of flakes.

This is in no way to be considered an in-depth study - but let me state that what follows are pretty basic rules that took me, John, quite a few years, and lotsa rocks, to figure out. Now I'm not one to ask much for directions ... I pretty well like to learn as much as I can by simply doin' and figurin' ... which slows me considerably for sure. I've been around several what should be considered advanced flintknappers over the years and have found that unless one asks, explanations usually don't come forth. Rare is the performer who explains without prodding what he or she is doing at each step. Many simply don't really want to appear to be showing off, acting as if they know more. And, as with specialists in all fields, most advanced 'knappers tend to forget the needs of the beginner.

The tips that follow aren't really for the beginner who hasn't mastered the removal of flakes according to the above rules - tho some just might glean something. Flintknapping is one of those skills where the rules can't come all at one time. You need to break a certain amount of rock - get the feel of what is happening at various stages - before you can even consider what questions to ask or what answers are needed. For example, at stage one (wherever that is), rules from stage two and beyond can be drawn out for you and you won't have the slightest comprehension of what is being illustrated. But after a certain amount of breaking, one day you'll be watching someone else 'knappin and see him or her do something ... and *BINGO*! ... you'll grasp instantly some simple aspect of what they are doing ... something that has been holding up your advancment to the next stage.

During the progression from beginner to advanced flintknapper there are several "stages" that one goes thru. Let me give you my thoughts of this progression.

Stage one would have to be where one begins to understand and become adept at predictably removing flakes as tools. I would call **stage two** when one begins to be able to leave behind a tool in rougher forms such as uniface (worked on one side only) axes and adzes. **Stage three** would be when a bi-facial (flakes from both sides) tool remains, width to thickness (w/t) ratio somewhere around three to one (3:1). **Stage four** would be when the 'knapper can turn out pieces that would truely qualify as knives and/or spear points over four inches long and 5:1 (w/t).

These stages I have come up with can only be taken as rough averages. I suppose we can call them main stages - there will be several sub-stages in between. Each individual will be different ... these are about the steps of my progression. Tho I began with pressure flaking, you'll note that it is not listed. Except for the setting up of platforms, pressure flaking should be saved for step four and beyond. Myself, I probably fit in somewhere between stage four and five ... and yes, I do pressure flake.

When I'm making a piece I generally don't have anything particular in mind for a finished product. My goal, or homework so to speak, is to turn the rock into as long, wide and thin a piece as possible. Only as I approach the end do I begin to shape it into a certain style. I don't replicate with replication in mind. I'm building my skills to make functional tools. By aiming for long, wide and thin now, I hope to be perfecting my work so that when afield and in need I'll be able to more easily come up with whatever tool I am in need of.

Coming to understand each of the following has helped *me* to improve considerably. I hope it's what you're needing.

Center line of mass. To remove long, thinning flakes from the piece, the striking surface needs to be on the same side, below the center line of mass, as the flake to be removed. (Note photo series towards end of chapter.)

The four flakes at left show how the energy wants to flow. The bulb of percussion (where it was hit) is on the right side. The ideal shape for running long flakes is curved, as seen in the familiar "arrowhead", lens shape of the pieces below.

Flakes don't like to run flat. If you look at any well defined flake, you'll note that it is not flat ... but that the flow of the energy *curls into* the parent rock. If the surface is flat and wide enough, the energy will likely terminate partways across the surface. A lens shaped surface is ideal for shooting a flake.

Flakes will want to follow old flake scar ridges. The ridge is a high spot on the stone. Remember, you cannot predictably remove more than one half of a cone in flintknapping (of course there are exceptions to about all rules) ... the ridge delineates less than half a cone.

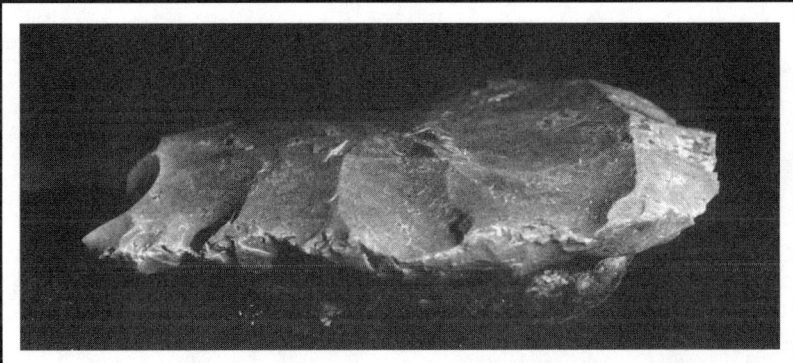

Ridge scars can be natural trails for flakes to follow.

Flakes will run longitudinally easier than straight across. A flake removed from a lens shaped piece will run further if taken at an angle to the center line because it has to bend less sharply.

When a flake terminates suddenly at or near the centerline of the piece, *remove flakes alternately*

141

Longer flakes can be driven over the center of the lens shaped piece if taken at an oblique angle rather than straight in as they need to bend less over the center line.

from opposite sides. I used to have a regular mountain range running down the center of my finished pieces. This helps.

You gotta make it thicker before you can make it thinner. Huh? But yes. This simply refers to the fact that you need enough substance at the edges to create a strong striking surface for flake removal. The longer the flake, the stronger needs be the platform. So to thin a piece further, you need to narrow it (thicken it as far as width to thickness ratio is concerned) by building stronger edges.

Support. Boy, did I break a lot of pieces prior to gaining the understanding that I now have (right or wrong) about support. Hold it this way, support this tighter here. More padding (above or below?). Huh? Then I watched a master on video. He was working a piece at least 15 inches long. He *held it lightly* in one hand and struck his well prepared platforms exactly ... removing long flakes at each blow. We thought that he was gonna try to read thru it! It was amazing. <u>NO</u> SUPPORT!!! Just well prepared striking surfaces, below the centerline of mass, and hit with pin point accuracy. When I adapted this to my work, the breakage dropped considerably. To be sure, many forms of support are needed in flintknapping ... I just had understood that when the big boys spoke of support, they meant that all times and all circumstances required it. I here found that in many instances, my supporting of the piece was keeping it from "going with the flow" of the energy - and if the piece don't flow, it won't bend, but will snap.

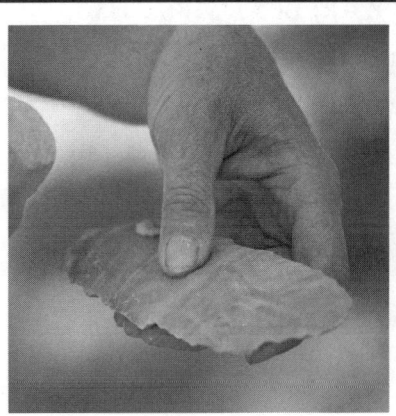

Striking while cradled in the hand (L) and well padded on the thigh (R). In both cases the piece is allowed to roll with the blow. The entire piece is in contact with the pad, even tho not tightly.

All of what I've talked about, both in our previous book and also here, is related to direct percussion, the striking directly of our "flint" rock with another stone ... usually referred to as *hard* percussion. The using of an antler for the striker is referred to as *soft* percussion. Soft percussion usually drives longer flakes.

Pressure flaking is simply the *pushing off* of flakes using such tools as antler tines (most common in days of old) or copper wire (most common today). I don't, and won't, spend much time instructing in this for beginners. Pressure flaking is used in the final stages of flintknapping. Most flintknappers, myself included, began by learning pressure flaking. It is a simple way to teach beginners, but not the best way for the student to learn flintknapping. The above rules apply here also.

To further your knowledge of flintknapping we recommend you refer to **"THE ART OF FLINTKNAPPING"** by D.C. Waldorf and **"FLINTKNAPPING, THE ART OF MAKING STONE TOOLS"** by Paul Hellweg.

My everyday tool kit: 2 hammerstones, 2 antler billets, two pressure flakers (1 each of copper and antler) and leather padding.

I once had a 'knapper tell me to expect an average of 10% of the stone to be left after finishing a piece. That's 90% reduction folks. Sounds like a lot, but let me tell you I feel fortunate to do that well most of the time. At left is one of my better, not average, attempts.

Typical primary flake removal, top side.

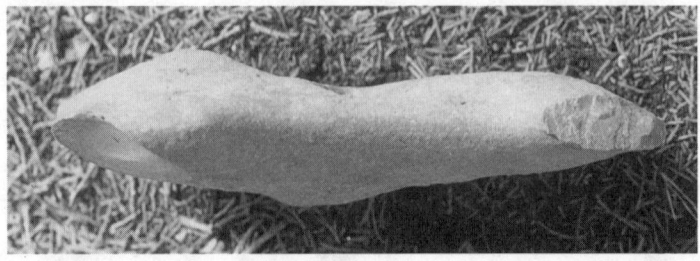

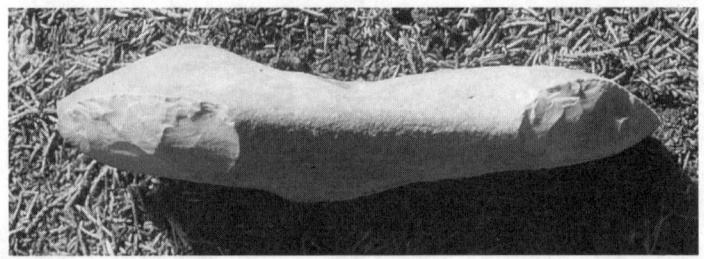

The photo sequence above illustrates how I first approach a "rock", in this case a cobble of Mill Creek chert. I always initially work to make the rock flat - this means I need to remove all high points to the level of the lowest. In the raw piece (top photo), you can clearly see three obvious high points. The second photo down shows the striking surfaces prepared to approach this, one on the left side and one on the right. Note that the prepared platforms are on the side that the flake is to be taken from. The bottom two photos show the flakes as they came off. These photos show the piece upside down as from when the flakes were removed. Refer to the photos on padding three pages back.

Secondary flake removal, same side.

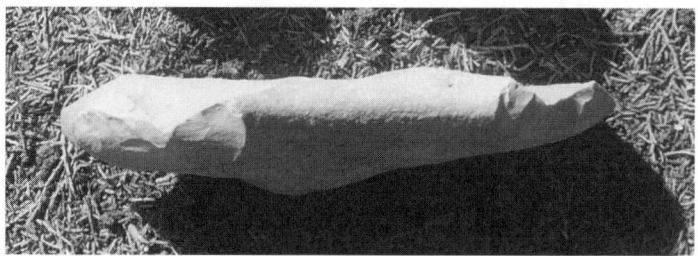

*Above, four additional platforms are set,
two on the left, two on the right.*

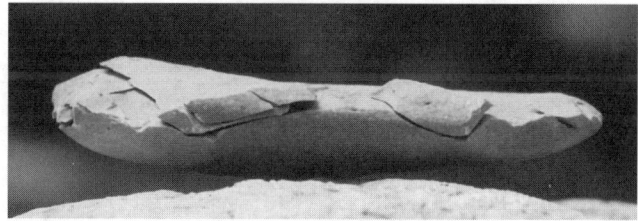

*These two middle photos show the
flakes removed in this series.*

*This last photo shows platforms prepared to begin removing flakes
from the other side.*

5 - B

LIGHTING

An assortment of primitive fat lamps. (Clockwise from top.) A hollowed out soapstone bowl, a clam shell, a turtle shell, a ceramic piece and a naturally hollow chunk of limestone.

*I*n a primitive situation there is no flashlight. Walking around in the dark can be somewhat hazardous at times, especially where there are limbs that want to poke your eyes out.

Most lighting for past primitives came from naturally tuned eyes. Night vision is something that moderns can develop also thru practice. Basically it's not much more than simply sitting in the dark for 30 minutes or so and letting the eyes adjust. You'll find that you will better discern things if you don't look directly at them. The periphereal vision comes into play here (something to do with rods and cones) and you can see things better by looking somewhat aside. The stars, and especially the moon, can provide enough light to get you around.

Around home, the campfire probably provided most light for past primitives, inside and out. But there were times when additional lighting was required and this was readily supplied by fat. Being flamable, fat made the ideal lighting fuel - sorta the kerosene of old.

If you got means of making fire, you've got the means of melting fat. Separating the meats & whatever will give a more pure fuel. The best results occur when the fat is heated slowly in a pot. Some add water for this (to prevent scorching?), we seldom do. Heat slowly and add more as needed. When all the fat is liquidfied, the oil, being lighter, will rise to the surface. This can be carefully poured off ... or if you wait until it cools you can then remove the entire mass from the container and scrape the trash from the bottom. The resulting tallow can be used for cooking, making pemmican (described in chapter four of NW-1) or for making lamps.

A hollowish stone, a clam shell or any other non-flamable container can be turned easily into a lighting fixture. Fill with tallow or fat, add a wick made from any p<u>lant</u> fiber that has been saturated with the same type oil, light and you got yourself a working lamp. The looser fibers, such as from the juniper, seem to work the best - absorbing fat and burning in what seems to be the right ratio. Eskimos used lamps like this for heat as well as lighting.

The simplest fat lamp that we have seen and used *(from Scientific American, March 1993)*, is a fist

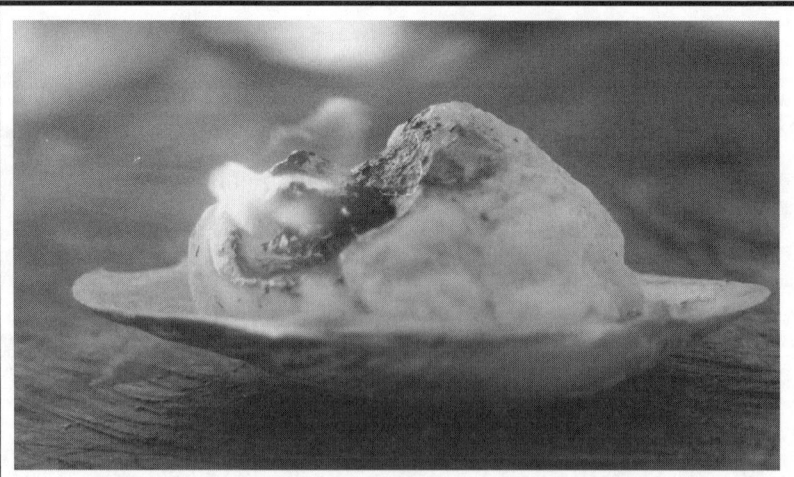

The easiest to make candle is simply a ball of raw fat into which a wick of natural fiber cordage is placed.

sized ball of plain old fat with wick inserted. Placed on a rock and you have an almost instant lighting fixture.

We keep two or more of these on hand when using them as they will eventually melt and the wick can drown in the liquid. When this is about to happen we just light the other, then put out the first.

The fat or tallow has a tendency to melt in the heat of the day in summer. This can be helped by adding bits and pieces of prickly pear cactus leaves while rendering. The resulting waxy surface stays firmer.

BONE NEEDLE

*T*here are several occasions in primitive living where the use of a needle is handy ... not so much in actual sewing of buckskin, as this is terrible hard, both on the bone needle and the buckskin, but around the household where everything is tied together in some manner.

We use needles in our everyday making of 'skins, but steel ones. The primitive way to sew buck- skin is to use a bone awl to make a hole, which will stay open (separated fibers) while you pass the hard pointed end of sinew thru it.

The most convenience that we have found for these bone needles is in sewing together cattails and tules in the making of mats.

Most bone is pretty brittle - here we are using the leg bone of a small sized deer - which has a thinner wall. We've heard that the leg bone of the coyote is more flexible.

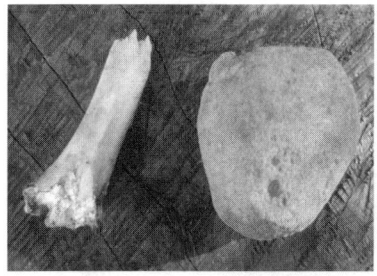

To start with you have to break the bone - some get fancier at this than we do - this works. Pick out as long and slender a piece as you want and have and make the hole first by gouging and drilling away at it with a sharp piece of flint-like rock.

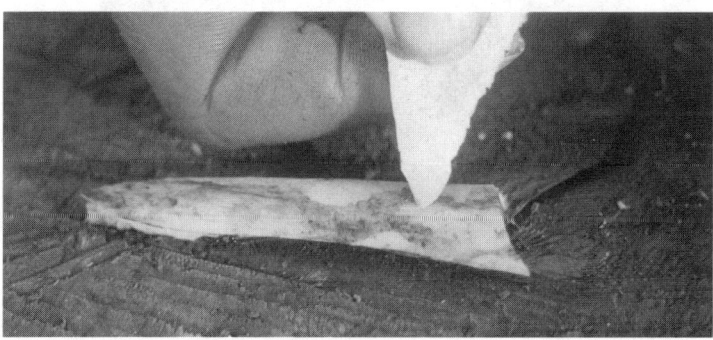

Grinding and smoothing with various grit sandstones will give you a shiny needle that fits the hole.

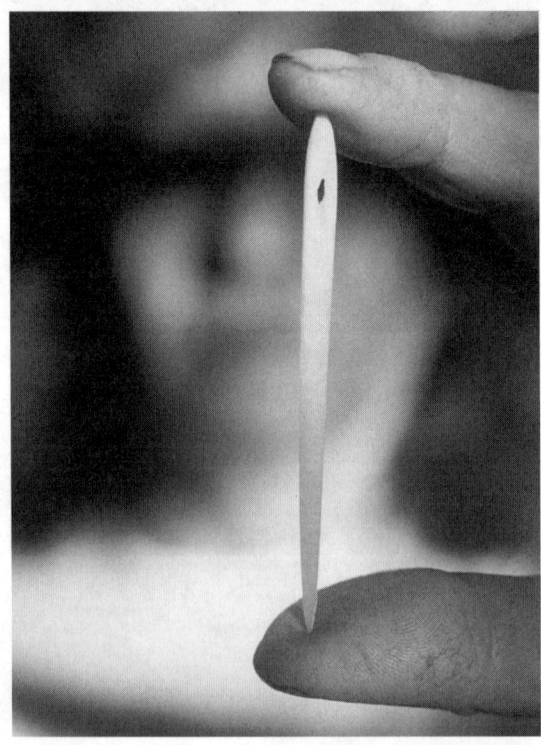

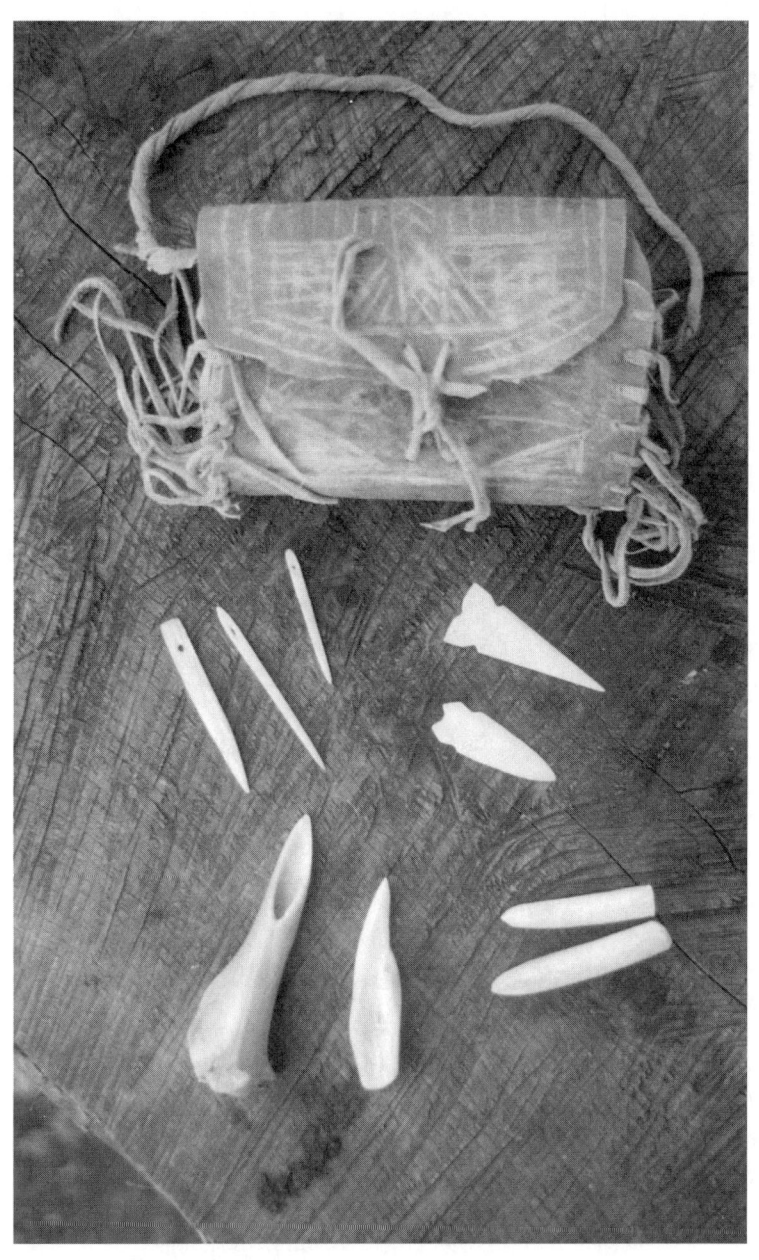

An assortment of bone awls, needles and
arrowpoints made by the same method.

Antler, as well as bone, makes for useful products. The above articles were made from split elk antler - by all primitive methods. Antler is easier to work with stone if it is moist heated first to soften it. This can cause some weakening of the substance if overdone ... tho with products such as the comb and snow goggles above it would make little or no difference.

5 -D
QUICK AX HAFTING

Mounting a stone ax onto a handle makes a chopping job much easier, but this usually requires a lot of time and effort. If the project that you're working on is short term, as in survival, then you want results fast. The next sub-chapter on, quickie bows, and also chapter 8 of this book cover another way than what we show here.

A semi-competent flintknapper can turn out this ax-head in a matter of only several minutes. It needs to be tapered so that the chopping itself will only help to make the fit tighter - as with a celt. The making of a length of durable cordage will take the same, or more, time.

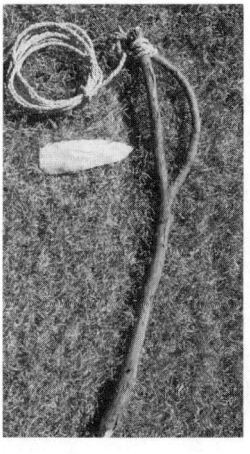

If the piece is overly lens shaped, placing a small stick on either side of the stone head will help to stabilize it. Here we wrap the stone in buckskin to prevent it from cutting the cord and also to create a cushioning. In the wild, a piece of pliable bark will work. Sometimes requiring fine tuning, this design does work well.

157

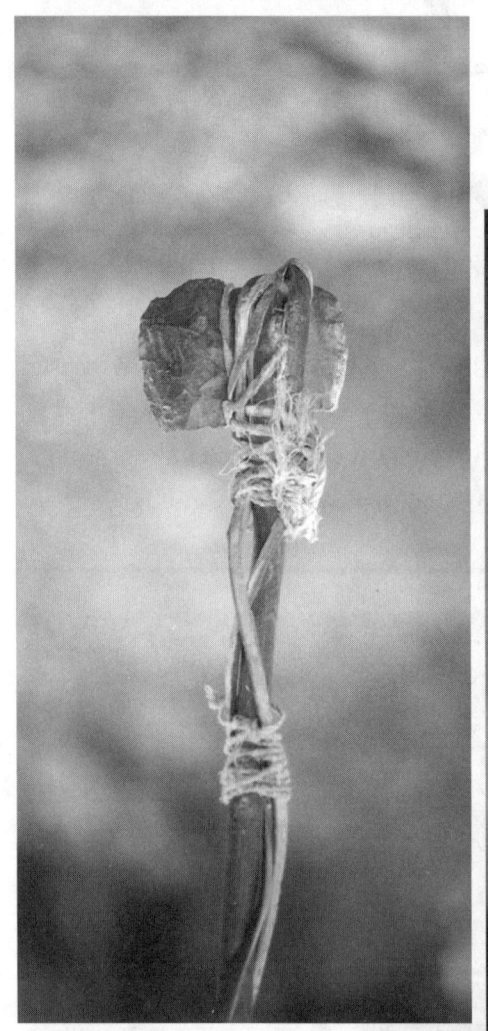

The ax on the left, above, was made in about a half hour several years back. A small green elm was cut off, split, the inside split removed and each of the remaining two quarters was then wrapped twice around the stone head. It's cut over 50 trees since then, most around two inches in diameter. The ax handle shown on the right was an experimental piece made at about the same time. Using a steel knife I spent right at three hours finding, shaping, heating (by boiling) and bending - it was allowed to cool before hafting. This handle finally broke but proved itself well enough that I use the design regularly.

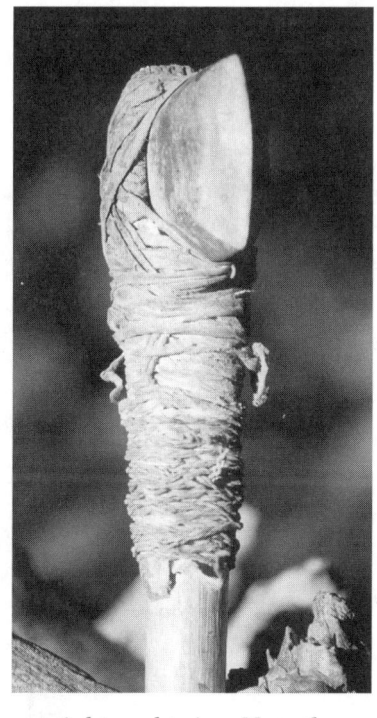

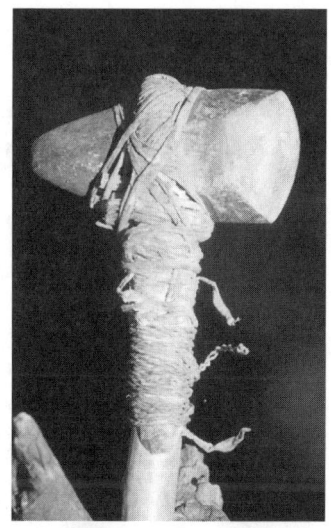

Two axes hafted using the previous method. The top one was made five years ago and has been in continuous service since, having been retightened twice. Note the wood wedges inserted to tighten things a bit. The lower ax was made two seasons back to use on the canoe. Note wrapping of rawhide where they bend around the top of the stones - this helps to reinforce as it wants to tear apart.

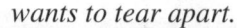

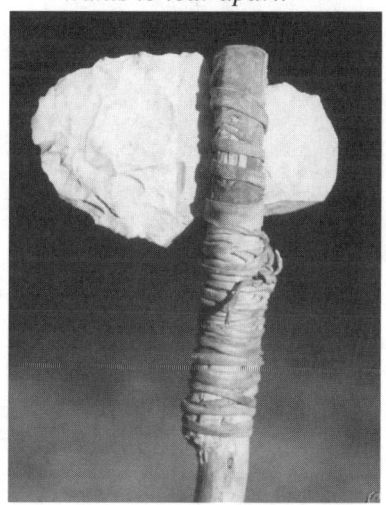

The
QUICKIE BOW

Maybe nothing to set records with, but even as negligible a wood as willow can produce a useful bow. These two examples are made from diamond willow from Montana - lightweight yes, but functional.

*B*ows are fun! While we don't recommend spending time on hunting in primitive or survival situations, having a bow along for taking opportunistic shots is a great idea.

In chapter eight I go into some depth on the physics of bow making (as well as in chapter three of NW-1). I won't do so again here. Chapter 8 also illustrates the making of a bow "right now" - a real quickie - from materials available. There we use two even sized limbs to make the two limbs of the bow. The same material can be used in making a self, one piece bow following those directions.

Here I will show how to make a bow in just a matter of days from green wood (initial inspiration for this comes from Jim Riggs). Making the "quickie" bow from green wood gives one the advantage of a wider selection of wood and design than when restricted to working with what happens to be available cured. It just takes a little longer.

Early last spring ('96), I was contacted about doing an article for the premier issue of INSTINTIVE ARCHER MAGAZINE. I passed the assignment along to Ivan who produced the following bow.

It all begins with the flaking out of an ax (above) and the making of a coupla pieces of cordage (R).

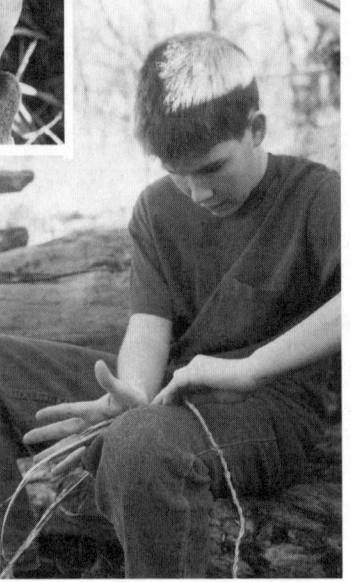

(Top & R) These are combined with small diameter, pliable sticks to make a usable hafted ax - all in less than 45 minutes.

(Top) The selected tree is chopped down and brought home, (L) split in two (having used antler and rock wedges) and (R) the bark is removed.

(L) The green piece is adzed into a rough bow, (below) tied onto a solid limb (with hand made cordage) and formed to desired shape where it will remain for up to a week when it is then (below L & R) final tillered.

Primitive, primitive
The result ... a snappy, 35# bow drawing a 26 inch arrow
... done from start to finish with primitive made primitive
tools.

5 -F

WATER CONTAINERS

Three examples of ceramic water containers. On the left is a quart sized, small mouth canteen with rawhide and buckskin carrier. The middle is a gallon container more suitable for use in an established camp. The right example is a half gallon canteen - somewhere at just too large for convenient carrying. The larger the carried ceramic vessel, the more liklihood is the breakage.

*O*ne aspect of primitive living that is sometimes overlooked is that of containers. In this day and age one takes it for granted that pockets are there ... and with some outdoor related clothes, BIG pockets. Primitively, or in many survival situations, pockets may not be there ... or if so, not in quantity or size to satisfy the needs.

The most overlooked container is probably the water bottle or canteen. Just how does one transport liquid? As in most primitive related questions one needs to look to the past for the answers.

In our book NW-1, we devote two entire chapters to containers. Several water containers are shown using animal parts (such as the bladder). When working with ceramics there are many styles and sizes that can be made.

Another pretty common jug that is available to the primitive is the basket covered with pine pitch. We have made and used these for several years now. The only real problem that we have had is having the pitch "flow" and settle on the finished product while stored in our house between uses. This has opened some leaks but a little time with the pitch pot has corrected this prior to use.

The pitch is mixed with powdered charcoal while heating it to create a more stable bond. The ratio between heat and time while melting the pitch can be critical ... too hot and too long makes for too brittle. The other extreme makes for too syrupy.

Willow basket (above) is being coated with pitch on the inside prior to closing up the opening. Not all of our pitch jugs have been coated on both sides ... and just coating the outside seems to work as well. The water takes on a sweet taste and is pleasant to drink - tho sometimes, as with this particular bottle, it is too much so. Note how the pitch has settled around the rawhide carrier straps in photo at left.

The rawhide water bucket above would serve just as well as a canteen if the top was made smaller. Simple and quick to make it requires only the skin of an animal. The egg below came from an ostrich - not too many here-abouts. This one holds over a quart.

Primitive Navigation

*A*bstract again? ... well, in ways, yes. Traveling, in the primitive situation will have to be defined a bit first.

We have to forget modern techniques ... in fact, in a sense we have to forget the modern world entirely and get ourselves into a primitive mindset ... as in days gone by. Bear with me a bit.

The primitive of old had things much different. He traveled unencumbered. He had no modern boundaries (fences, roads, towns, farms, et al) to impede - or to guide - his way. The primitive of old pretty much traveled in a circle - a seasonal circle. He wintered in a sheltered location that would provide relief from the weather and had ample food supplies. The rest of the year found him wandering in search of life's other necessities; flint, plant foods, fibers, clay, bow or other wooden implement sources, fishing locations, and on and on. The circle that was traveled was known to the family/group and landmarks and watersheds pretty well served to show the way - his map as it was. Sure he had the need to know north from west from south from east - but in a limited way.

So lets us try to convert some of this type

thinking of yesterday to today in a mostly dreamed of situation - a place far from any contact with modern man or his ways. Remember, the only places that are really remote enough in this modern world of ours to qualify would be, for the most part, too harsh for man to live - the reason that it's untouched.

Take away all man made things and how is the earth broken up or divided? ... into watersheds. Water flows downhill. Rain falling on one side of a hill or ridge way well end up thousands of miles away from rain falling just feet away on the other side. It just depends on the lay of the land. This is the basic map - it's how the earliest explorers found their way around ... and how they told the next person how to get to any particular place.

"Head up this river until the first major river of almost the same size coming in from the right hand side - about six days easy travel by foot. Then follow that river to the third creek wider than two men are tall - that comes in from the left, about one day of easy travel. Just to the left of that junction, on the second hilltop on your left, you will find our village." Old timey directions from the Kansas river junction with the Missouri river to our place. Can't get much simpler than that.

Water runs downhill. It don't always run to the same spot. Certainly not by the same route. We like to study the lay of the land on our cross country jaunts and play around with the question of "if it rained five inches here, where would it go?" One pretty quickly begins to *read* the land. You just have to mentally wipe out the roads. Make the water courses your highways.

Secondly, watch for unusual formations or sites that can be seen from a distance. Lots of miles can be saved ... as in, "follow this river for about three days travel and when you see the point of the chimney rock to the right front of where you are heading, the tall pointed one, not the squat flat-top one, head directly towards it." Maybe the river course will twist and turn in such a manner that you would spend several extra days following it.

Most assuredly compass directions were used. But with no real compasses and maps to guide one accurately, what is the *true* direction west. The sun sets in the west - or something like a westerly direction. In summer it's north of west - in winter, south. The accuracy of the sun-stick compass (as illustrated) is only just so accurate - exactly east to west only if you mark during mid-day. And if the sun ain't shining at that time of day, especially for days at a time, it don't mean much. If the directions are WEST, then you had better be heading WEST. Not a little north or south. Directions by watercourses and landmarks wouldn't be quite so haphazard.

But to the modern day abo who has found his spot. You just can't travel in the circle of the old - at best you'll most likely end up in jail. Find a spot that contains the resources that you need. If you got a sheltered home site and most resources, stay there. You gotta or wanta travel?, ... use the watercourses and landmarks to guide you. WATCH YOU BACKTRAIL. You have to be able to see what it looks like from the direction that you will be traveling on the way home. It does look different.

> *If you don't know where you are,*
> *you won't know which direction to travel ...*
> *a compass would be useless.*

If you don't know where you are or what is out there, a compass will do you know good at all. I mean, what good does it do you to know which direction is east if you

172

have no idea at all what is there. But lets say you have a camp on a watercourse and you have the desire to explore for resources. You know that the river runs basically north/south for some distance (for the modern day hiker, this could be a road). There are no major landmarks. You head away from the river and you will be traveling either east or west. The river (or road) can be found again if you can figure out any one of the directions and travel in reverse. There are several ways that you can do this, some more accurate than others. Knowing where your camp is once you get back to the river would depend on just how aware you were heading out. Did you head in a more northerly or southerly direction?

The method most touted in primitive navigation circles is where a stick is stuck in the ground and the shadow of the point is tracked. A good and reliable system. A mark of some sort is placed where the shadow of the tip of the stick falls. Fifteen to 30 minutes later another. Since the sun rises in the east and sets in the west, this gives you an west/east line ... *kinda*. The shorter the space between evenly timed marks, the closer to solar noon it is. When the shadow is shortest(solar noon) it will be pointing due north.

Great! But ... !

Many go wrong in describing this method by stating that the shadow points are always east/west. This is not so. The line of the shadow will track east/west during the entire day **only twice a year**. Only twice, once in the spring and again in the fall, on the equinoxes, does the sun travel directly east to west during the entire day. At the winter and summer equinox the line will be a pretty exaggerated half egg shape. And this can surely screw you up.

Note the drawing here. These marks were made in mid October. This is less than one month from the fall equinox. That's over two full months from **full** distortion!

173

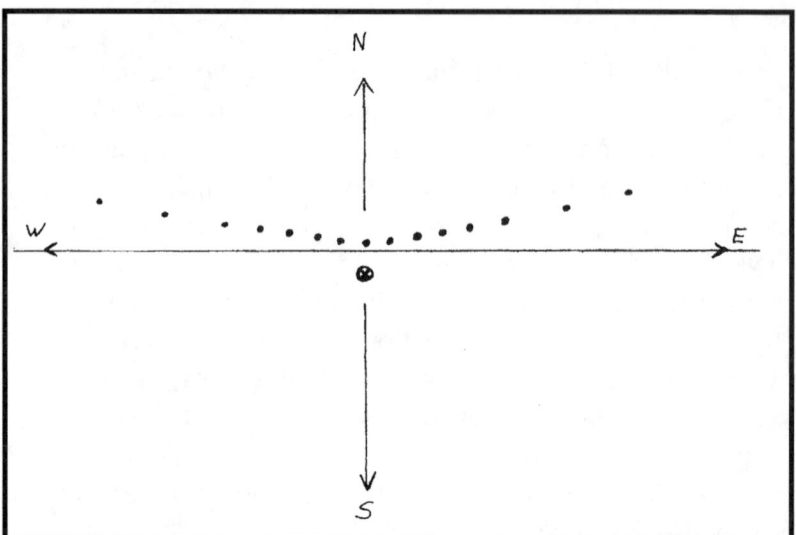

The above sun/stick compass chart was made in mid October. The dots are marks placed at 30 minute intervals beginning in early morning. Tho marks were made before and after those shown, they here would be off the page because of the length-ened shadows. This illustration covers 3 1/2 hours both before and after solar noon. The east-west line was determined by drawing a line between any two equal marks either side of the noon mark, which is marked with the shortest shadow. A line from the stick to the noon mark is directly north/south.

The east west line is close to ten degrees off for seven hours - from 0930 to 1300 (solar noon) and from 1300 to 1630. Ten degrees is a lot, folks. Before and after these times, it falls even more. (This reading was taken again just two weeks later - as we were going to press - and the variation was up to 16 degrees.) The only exact line will be drawn from equal times before and after solar noon ... that is, a line drawn from the shadow marks 30 minutes before and 30 minutes (or whatever duration) after solar noon will be exactly east to west. Since you must pass solar noon to determine this exactly, it becomes redundant as solar noon is due

north. East/west can be determined by this. Three hours
before and after solar noon, the line begins to swerve
even more, in this case, to the north.

In the winter, the sun rises and sets south of east
and west. During the summer this is reversed, the sun
rising and setting north of east/west.

Now this don't make this system wrong. One
just needs to be aware. When one doesn't have modern
trappings to point the way, one becomes aware. Kinda
like night vision. It just needs to be developed. The
primitive knew (and knows) the seasons. He instinc-
tively knows mid-day without the stick. He knows how
long it has been since the sun rose and how long before
it sets. This is all sorted in his computer system, the
brain, and he can travel in the direction he desires
simply by knowing where the sun is. Traveling westerly, the sun will be behind the left shoulder in the
morning. The closer to mid-day it gets, the sun will be
more immediately to the left of the observer and as the
afternoon goes on the sun will move towards the left
front. The true, aware, primitive doesn't need the sticks.
(Probably the closest that most moderns can relate to
this is by going without a watch for an extended period.
After just a few months you should be able to give the
time accurately to within minutes. I know the time at
night when I awake to go to the bathroom.)

If the sun don't shine? Well, unless you've got a
landmark, you're gonna hafta kinda wing it. If the
moon and stars are visible at night you can also find the
directions. The moon rises east'ish and sets west'ish ...
it follows the sun's path within just a few degrees.
Instead of a stick in the ground to track the shadow,
here you'll need to use two points between you and the
moon such as tree limbs or tall rocks. Lay down looking up at a point where the moon is behind an object,

175

The North Star, Polaris, is center ... the tail star of the little dipper , which can be difficult to locate as these are dim stars. The Big Dipper, left, is more easily located. Two stars forming the dipper's edge point somewhat towards Polaris, which is the brightest star in that immediate area. The North Star pretty much stays in one place as the rest of the stars circle it (actually the Earth spinning). When the Big Dipper is low in the northern sky and you are in timbered or hilly country, it can sometimes be difficult to locate - fortunately the prominent distorted "W", Cassiopeia, will then be visible to act as a guide.

say a solid tree limb, and follow it till it hides behind another. Make a mental note (or better yet, write it down). Place a rock where you head rested and go to sleep. When daylight comes it shouldn't take you too much figuring to determine east/west.

The north star (Polaris) is pretty much north. Knowing just two readily identifiable, easy to discern constellations can show you where the north star is. The big dipper somewhat points to Polaris from one direction, Cassiopeia from the opposite (note drawing). If the day is cloudy and it clears some during the night, you can get guidance.

Still cloudy? Some generalities. Here in mid-America, in the summer the wind is mostly from the south, usually from the southwest, less often from the southeast. Just prior to a storm the wind is usually drawn into the storm front from the east.

During the winter months the wind is mostly from the north, again generally from a westerly direction. If it's December and the wind is warm? Likely a southerly wind.

Don't rely on which side of the tree moss is growing on.

During the winter months the snow will be maybe somewhat less deep, with more bare ground patches showing, on the south sides of hills - or large rocks or trees - because the sun will be hitting it more during the days and if it doesn't actually melt the snow, it can cause it to settle more than where the sun don't reach. If the snow surface is hard from thawing and freezing and you find patches where it is still fluffy, it will most assuredly be on the north side of something.

> *If you have all your needs satisfied*
> *at or near your home camp,*
> *why leave?*

So what have we concluded here? I guess one main point is that the modern primitive should stay at home. If he has all he needs, why leave? As one branches out from his home base over time, landmarks, mainly in the form of watersheds, will become familiar to her/him and for miles around he'll know exactly where he is in relation to home. If there is no home and the territory is unfamiliar, what's the big deal in traveling in one direction over another? If she don't know what's where, what's the difference? Oh well, just some more to think about.

Two piece moccasins

Heavy duty, brain tanned elkhide, two piece moccasins.

*I*n most things that we do, we try to figure the easiest and least time consuming method. Not so in the making of our everyday moccasins.

There are several illustrated, easy, kinda one step, patterns available for turning one's freshly tanned buckskin into footwear - Jim Rigg's in his book "Blue Mountain Buckskin" and Randal Jones' "Perfect 15-minute Moccasin" in **WILDERNESS WAY**, volume 1, Issue #3 *(POB 203, Lufkin, TX 75902-0203)* , are just two readily accessible. We show you in chapter 9 of this book probably the fastest moccasin around ... but ... our personal favorite primitive footwear is the Plains Indian style two piece moccasin.

This style can be a real pain to put together to fit your foot properly, but once done we feel that, if nothing else, it is the best lookin' of the moccosins around. And tho we really like the comfort afforded by these, they are probably no better than the others mentioned. *The Plains Indians really liked them* as is attested to by a visit to any museum.

I have built these for many years now ... in fact, except for quickie, survival type situations, this is the only style I have made. You'd think I'd have it down pat by now. Not so! There are a lot of rules that you need to follow to get these to fit your feet properly. If you don't, they'll kinda just twist around on your foor like a mean spirited centipede.

Footwear of some type is pretty important in any survival or wilderness outing. It better be durable and comfortable or you'll end up on the disabled list.

The big difference between the plains style and other moccasins is that the plains style has the sole sewn on separately. Both buckskin and rawhide can be (and was) used for the soles. We primarily use buckskin. Up to now, the buckskin we had made our foorwear from was just that, buckskin ... from our local deer. We've used the thickest, toughest bucks we got. The heavier, the more durable and comfortable. The necks, usually the heaviest portion, is used for the soles.

We have made these using rawhide for the soles. Rawhide will wear longer than buckskin and protect the feet better ... but. The rawhide needs to be soaked to make for easier sewing - sewing swells the rawhide - getting it to fit exactly is tough. What we more commonly have done was to use the heavier portions from the deer and buffalo & elk when we had it. This we allowed to only partially tan - the outsides were soft but the middle was still kinda rawhide. This will last longer than the buckskin. The soles of these can and are replaced regularly as needed. The rough surface of buckskin grabs surfaces better than rawhide under any condition - but when it's wet out, then rawhide on grass or leaves is like skates on ice. Watch out! I learned this first while bow hunting in moccasins back in 1973. *Whoops!*

So, one may ask, why use rawhide at all - especially if your feet get pretty toughened when used outdoors regularly? Well, you only have to step in a patch of prickly pear cactus once in buckskin soles. Camped up Paradise Valley in Montana during the '88 national rendezvous I learned this first hand while running towards the "pie lady". Geri got the pie - I spent the rest of the evening pulling thorns outta my foot. I knew this at the time - it's just that I was wearing one of my plain buckskin soled pairs instead of a stiffer half done one (we have both).

The very simplest of solutions to this situation is an insole of rawhide.

All this buildup to illustrate here Geri's sure fire, two piece moccasin making recipe. She remembers how to do whatever it is I seem to do wrong a lot as I seldom get good fitting results the first try.

A hearty thanx to Bart and Robin Blankenship for their gift to us of the finely tanned elk that we turned into two pairs of mocs. *Bart & Robin offer courses geared to the beginner or the advanced abo from somewhere in Colorado (used to be Boulder but now they're building elsewhere). They also offer their knowledge thru their new book "EARTHKNACK, STONE AGE SKILLS FOR THE 21ST CENTURY" - for $14.95 plus, I would imagine, something for shipping. Address? Last we have, current as of this writing, is POB 19693, Boulder, CO 80308.*

(Next page) The making of the pattern is the first trick to get right . Make an outline of one of your bare feet (or with socks if you'll be wearing them) on paper - Geri prefers that the full standing body weight be on it ... then add a "bit" all the way around (for the seam) ... finally smooth the outside shape to more of an oval. The foot tracing illustrated is more bulbous because I have pretty prenounced bunions. The pattern is then placed on the buckskin to make it go as far as possible - if you've tanned this yourself you'll understand wanting to use buckskin sparingly.

The lower photo shows all cut pieces - two soles, two uppers and two tongues. The darker colored strips are thinner buckskin that will be placed between the seams as welts to help protect the stitching from wear.

The uppers are traced, as seen by the pencil mark in the upper photo, using the sole as a guide. Not so wide at the toe where it doesn't have to go as high, a bit wider at midsole where it must go over the center of the foot and widest at the back where it comes up to the ankle (or as high as you want). You'll note that the upper comes back a bit much beyond the ankle end. This insures that there is enough material - better too much than too little. You will eventually cut this off - if there is too much, as here, they can be made into the tongues. If too little, then you gotta start over.

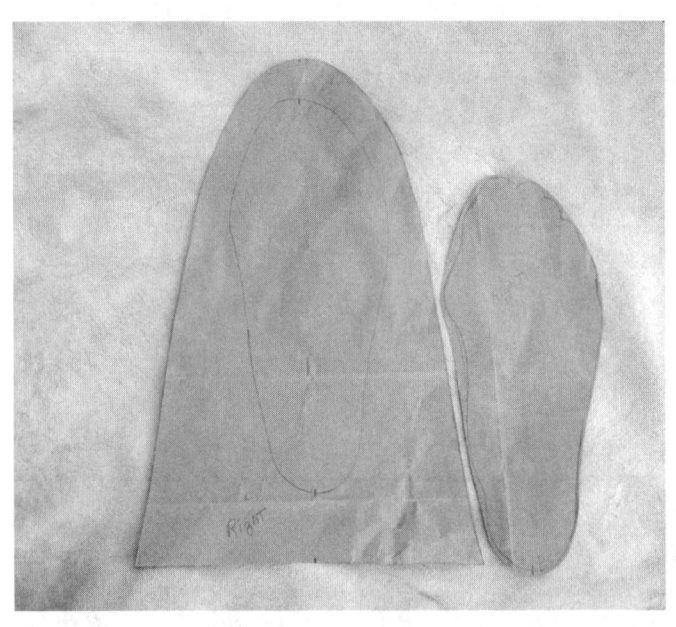

*Paper pattern (above) and
cut elk pieces (below).*

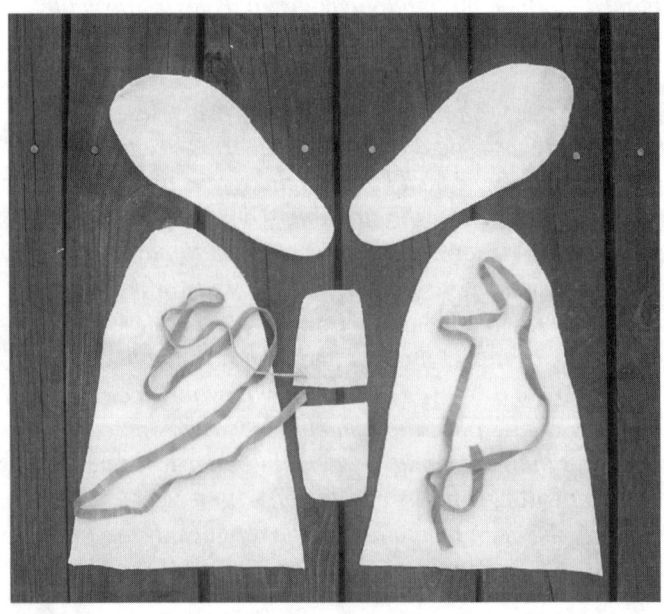

Begin sewing the upper to the sole at the midpoint of the toes. Go first one direction to the middle of the heel, and then the other. Do this with the moccasin inside out. Place the welt between the pieces to be sewn if you want -
this is not a necessity.

Before you will be able to invert the moccasin right side out you'll have to cut along the top the opening for the foot. To find this, note a line from the middle of the toe to the center of the upper at the ankle end. Cut just a bit at a time so that you don't over-do it. The final cut will be approximately one third the distance from the ankle - whatever fits
your foot.

Once inverted, place it on your foot and cut at right angles to this (note photos next page) a line to fit the tongue. This is determined by the fit of the moccasin to the foot. Once this is done, put your foot in and stand so that your leg is upright and pinch where the **top of the back fits to your ankle**. *Mark this spot, make a line, cut off the excess and*
sew the two ends together.

Sew the tongue on. Punch holes with an awl for the drawstrings and you're finished. (The drawstring is always inserted so that it goes around the ankle **on the outside of the moccasin** *and comes* **out at the front** *on either side from where you'll tie it.)*

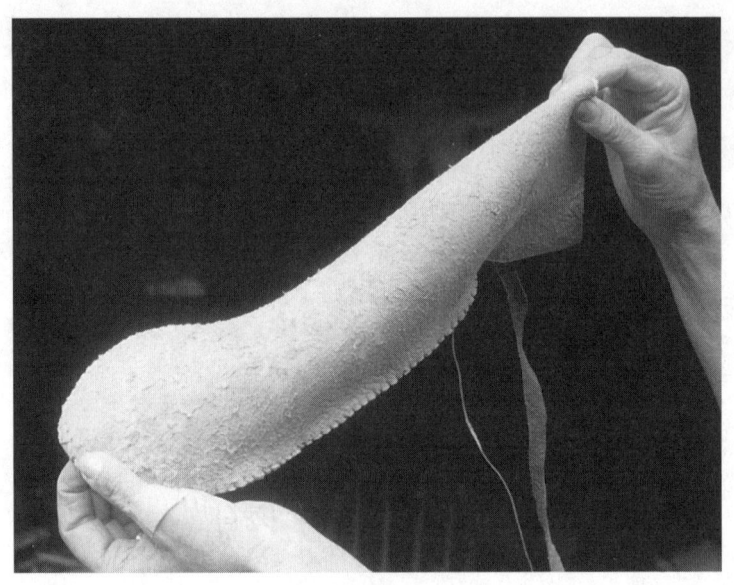

Finding the line running lengthwise (upper) in preparation to cut opening .
Inverted with heel line marked prior to cutting (below). The tongue is shown in place where cross line was cut.

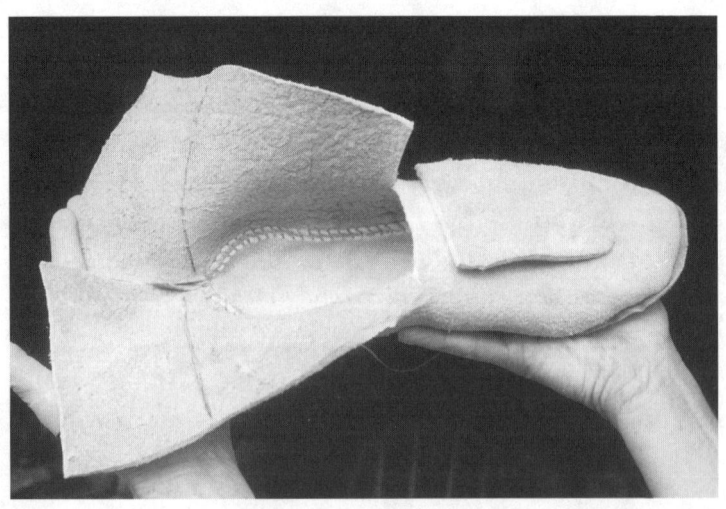

Finished moccasins with lightweight rawhide insoles.

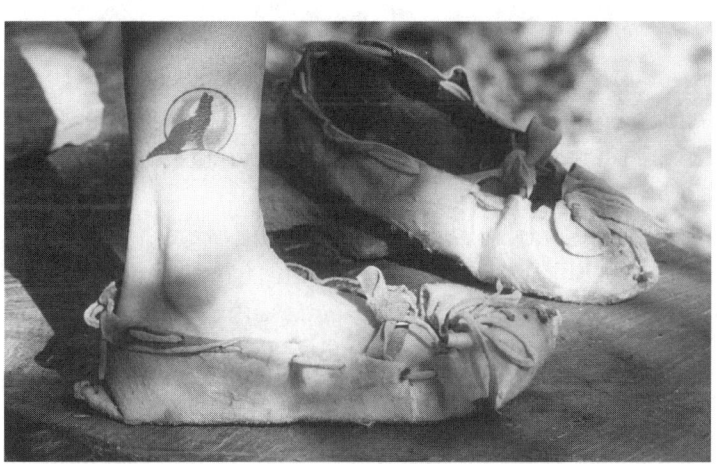

From Ireland comes another instant piece of footwear ...
pampooties ... common along the rocky coasts where ordinary
footwear wouldn't hold up. Simply a piece of heavy raw hide, the
hair was left on the outside to absorb most of the abuse and give
traction. Geri put the hair in, on these made from buffalo, for
comfort. They need to be kept wet or they will tear the feet up.

Primitive versus Prehistoric

I had planned approaching this subject in this book for some time - and then dropped the idea because most likely the majority of you readers don't really care about word games.

As most of you are becoming aware, there are a lot of people out there interested in what we call, *primitive* skills. But politics and political correctness among some "groups" of abo's around the country, seems to be important.

Why do we bring it up now? Well, another letter, this from a group in Scotland, saying that they prefer the word prehistoric to describe what they are doing because primitive *"suggests something rather basic and poorly made, which is often not the case"*.

Let's see what the Oxford American Dictionary has to say about this.

Prehistoric. *1. of the ancient period before written records of events were made. 2.* (informal) *completely out of this date.*

Primitive. *1. of or at an early stage of civilization,* primitive tribes. *2. simple or crude using unsophisticated techniques,* primitive tools.

I'm hoping not to expend too much energy on this, subject but lets explore it just a bit. Using definition #1 of prehistoric, *of the ancient period before written records of events were made,* how does one explain the American Natives. They were stone age until the arrival of Columbus - and then some. But Columbus had written records. So that makes me wonder, **who's** written records are we referring to. Ours? ... or theirs? And many cultures were using these "primitive" methods in their everyday lives long after having developed written records of their own ... Eastern (as in China), Mid-Eastern, South American (as in Maya & Aztec), Egyptian. And the Native Americans that met Columbus had their own rocords written out - it's just that they were, how shall I say it, - primitive. Hmmmmm!

As for description #2, *completely out of this date.* What date? There are yet today peoples using various primitive methods in their day to day lives - archery, dugouts, cordage, pottery, etc.

#1 of primitive ... *at an early stage of civilization.* Yeah! ... as Scott Silsby is fond of saying, "first, not worst".

#2 ... Simple, crude, using unsophistigated techniques. Yep, again.

Just what is meant by crude? ... simple? ... unsophistigated? Everything that we have written about and teach is exactly that ... *how to head to the out of doors and make for yourself something from nothing.* And we take a great amount of pride in just that crude, simple, unsophisticated jewel that we have created ourselves from what nature has offered us - using nothing but the same as tools. Take for example the dugout canoe featured in chapter four - including just about all of the tools that were used in its creation. A few people who have had the opportunity to admire this have asked about all of the unevenness and marks left behind. One suggested sanding it smooth. Huh? Hey, we're awfully proud of every mark that is showing on this canoe. Each and every one made by hand using a primitively made stone tool. A final step in the making of aboriginal dugouts was to scorch the entire thing - charring helps to preserve the wood. We have elected not to do this as we're afraid that some, if not all, of the tool marks would be lost.

And while I'm on the subject of politics - would you believe that we have seen in print that some people seem to think that there should be rules to govern people doing just the sort of stuff that we are writing about? Duh!

Talk about big government.

Fini.

Chapter
6

PRIMITIVE, PRIMITIVE

Ivan and Geri strip yucca leaves for ties in putting up our traveling Primitive, Primitive shelter.

A term coined by us in an interview with Practical Survival magazine in 1991, *primitive, primitive* refers to doing a project or skill using nothing but natural items and tools from start to finish. (We have seen this term used in print by others since.)

Our primitive campsite - here set up while teaching in Colorado. The shelter frame is tied together with natural fibers ... this in turn has been covered with slough grass and cattail mats ... all tied down with a 60 foot, six ply, natural fiber rope.

Now, throughout this chapter I'll be referring specifically to accomplishing tasks at hand using nothing but primitive methods ... but let me make a coupla statements right off;

1) We are not belittling those who make it a practice of producing primitive products utilizing modern technology - as in bow makers using bandsaws, et al. It's just that in *our* approach to primitive skills, we look at the overall picture - as in how one could not just survive but actually live pretty comfortably under strictly primitive conditions. This requires the knowledge of <u>an entire circle of skills</u>.

2) In almost all of our instructions and in much of our everyday practice and research of primitive skills *we do* use steel tools; in our intensive two weeks skills courses that we used to conduct, our students became proficient in most aspects of daily primitive living ... including bowmaking and making and using stone tools. *If we were to teach a student how to make a bow using nothing but the primitive tools that he had made, this alone would take most of the two weeks.* So, I guess what I'm trying to say here is that tho we do make and use stone and other natural tools in all aspects of all of our primitive living skills and projects, we do not use them in every project we do.

•

This chapter is just a mish-mash. Ideas, shortcuts, things on my mind ... whatever.

The following three chapters center around how one can actually head "Naked into the Wilderness" and accomplish any of a number of tasks or skills. They are not written as "how-to's", but there is a lot of how-to in them. The purpose is not necessarily to show you "how" to accomplish certain tasks but to illustrate just how these skills would fit into the daily regimen of primitive living.

(Note - I have twice seen it in print, in "how-to" outdoor survival skills books, that friction fire cannot be made on the spot in the wilderness except under the very best of conditions. Poppycock! Here we regularly make friction fire in the wild using nothing but primitive, primitive methods - sometimes in the mist, on occassion immediately following rains - and there are several others around who are fully as capable.)

To actually live a primitive life-style one needs

A true primitive pot cannot be made without the primitive fire.

to know and understand an entire spectrum of skills. It's not enough to know how to make a bow ... or to tan a skin ... or to make a pot. These and many other projects are *advanced living* skills and they require the knowledge of many other basic skills. You can't make a primitive pot without knowing how to make a primitive fire. A bow will do you no good without a string.

Now take note that we have been speaking of skills. At a gathering that we once taught at, a young lady, seemingly confused, asked of us, "just what are the priorities in this primitive field?". In one area of the grounds, basic flintknapping was being taught. Over there was a fellow teaching bow making. Someone else was teaching how to make and use natural dyes. Another how to felt wool. Another was telling stories. Another how to make drums. Tanning was touched on. Bags were being netted. Most of the instructors were specialists in only their particulair field. She posed a good and valid question, one that many beginning primitives need to face.

Abstract. *Theoretical rather than practical*. As discussed earlier, a pretty good description to what we're into. I mean, I don't know of and have not heard of anyone in this day and age who lives and breathes primitive, primitive 100%. The very closest would have to be aborigines isolated from most day to day contact with the outside world. And *they* have and use steel tools. This ain't no game for them. It's one heck of a lot easier to dig out a log for a canoe using steel tools rather than stone (something we know from experience). Can you picture some aboriginal anywhere in the world shopping for a *stone* ax or adze to refine his canoe to *make it pure*. Face it. Steel is easier.

I remember one time, Larry Dean Olsen, an early instructor of primitive, was squatted around our campfire enthralling a small audience with tales of his adventures. He has spent thousands of hours (or more) running the deserts with students. As a lull occurred in the conversation, I asked him, "Larry, have you ever run across anyone who actually lives the life"?

"What", says he, "do you mean?"

"Well", I ventured, "we're all just *playing* at this. Have you ever run across anyone who actually lives it"?

Silence. I don't recall any answer but I do recall the silence.

Big names in this field, or just anyone who spends the majority of their time practicing primitive, don't want it to be considered games. *We* sure don't think of it as games.

But it sure is abstract. So lets pursue this train of thought for a bit.

Geri and I spend just about every moment of every day "primitive". As I sit here at my computer writing this piece on *primitive*, (Geri has hers also - with which she is writing a novel about the stone age -

both are powered by solar as we have no electricity),
Geri is down below working on a ceramic pot and a 13
year old protege is out front using a stone adze to
fashion a paddle from a tree he cut down with a stone

*Using a primitively made stone ax, Ivan fells a cedar
tree to fashion into a paddle.*

A stone adze (above) is used to rough shape the cedar into a fully functional paddle (below).

ax to power the dugout canoe that we are in the process of finishing off (begun last year as a 30 inch diameter cottonwood tree) ... all done with stone tools. We have been spending the better part of every day since summer began working on this project. Mornings are usually spent actually working on the dugout and the afternoons, when necessary, are used for repairing and upkeep of tools ... 90% of which are made with stone tools including the holes drilled (hand drills with stone bits) into cured osage orange for an Eskimo type adze and the hand drill fire used to burn holes in the celt handles.

(Note - From my personal experience, flaked flint type axes and adzes work as good, or better, than ground tools - with much less time and effort involved in the construction there-of.)

In between, I write this, answer questions received in the mail (yes, we do answer questions), *mail* out copies of our books and tapes. We drive to the post office in our *pickup* - do our cooking over a *propane range*, wear typical *modern clothes* (blue jeans and "T" shirt mostly). Our *phone* rings pretty regularly. A *chain saw* helps us out with the winter's firewood.

Then take the couple that many modern primitives are aware of, Matt 'n Molly, who had lived primitively in NW Montana with their two children, who were born *out there*. They lived about as primitively as any we know. Having had their children in the bush (or close anyhow), living in buckskins they tanned themselves, feeding themselves daily from what nature offers. They tanned extra buckskins to *sell* for a cash flow. They had a *vehicle*. They had *bought land* (taxes go with land ownership). They cooked with *cast iron*, lived in a *canvas* tent, used *steel tools* regularly in their day to day living. These people spent just about every moment of every day "primitive".

Who, or what, is right? Face it, we all make and justify our own rules.

•

So, what about the skills? Well, we consider that there are five basic skills that one needs as a pool. All other skills derive from these.

1) Fire, 2) cordage, 3) traps, 4) tools and 5) shelters. *Fire* not only comforts but is a tool. *Cordage* is vital in many projects including many *traps* which is what will be feeding you. *Tools*, most notably a sharp cutting edge of stone, are required for just about all projects. *Shelter* will protect you from the elements.

If you were to use the term survival, these are the basics to have down. Being proficient in these can save your life. The basics. Most other skills or projects reguire the use of one or more of these. So, if one desires to be a well rounded, all American Abo (ab-original), this is where to begin. ***Get a good grasp of the basic skills***.

If someday, for whatever *abstract* reason, you were to *want* to place yourself in a long term primitive living situation, then you would certainly want to add to this list. Tanning, pottery, bows (& arrows), more & better methods of food procurement, containers (& more containers), cooking skills, navigation, biology, geology. The list is long. *Of skills.* This is what I want

The stone tool can be as simple as the flakes (above, at left) or more refined into an ax or adze (above R). Hafted blades add much convenience to the tool kit. (Below L) A flaked flint celt is set into a handle of which the hole has been burned - the fire begun with a hand drill. The Eskimo style adze (below R) was burned to length with same fire and holes were drilled into the cured osage handle with flint tipped hand drills.

to stress. *Skills.*

So, you see from the way that we look at it, it's all abstract.

But if your abstractness is leading you towards some freedom of dependency (this *is* the ultimate in self-sufficiency), learning how to stay alive in the wilderness (our world minus all man-made extras) is a very real need. Face it, if you can't stay alive, there's nothing to live for. And what will keep you alive are the basic skills mentioned earlier. To live comfortably, the *advanced* living skills come into play.

Now that I've talked primitive, primitive being abstract - lets talk about abstract versus ...

Abstract, abstract.

Of the number of people whom we've come into contact with over the years in this field (many thousands), in our opinion, only a very small handful would qualify as being capable of actually heading "naked into the wilderness" with any chance at all of surviving even the first week, much less any extended period of living.

A handful out of thousands ... Why?

Well, it's because there's just too much emphasis placed on what we refer to as *woo-woo*. (Not our term, but borrowed from an article along these same lines.)

Head to any primitive gathering. Look at many books on this subject. Encounter just about any man on the street who is into primitive life-styles. Where do you find the majority of people and time spent? On basic non-essentials.

An expert flintknapper visited here just weeks ago and commented on one of the more popular primitive gatherings that he had attended. He said that he had less than five people learning what he had to offer at one of his presentations on flintknapping and that the fellow teaching the making of cattail dolls had a herd of people surrounding him. *C'mon now.*

•

Edible and medicinal plants. As covered in more detail in chapter two, fine as a supplement and

The simple modified paiute deadfall shown here can be learned in just minutes and takes no longer to set.

learn as much as you can about them as you go - but a true vegetarian just won't make it out there (unless she's in the tropics). You can learn a simple trap in minutes - eating the entire animal will supply your bodily needs with a minimum of expended calories on your part. It takes a lot less training to learn what parts of what animals not to eat than to learn the same about plants.

Camouflage. Well, in Viet Nam I depended on it. Here I have had deer and other game approach me within easy bow or handgun (spear?) range while I was wearing hunter orange. Be aware of wind direction (work into it), making little noise (you can't make none - even the wind makes sound), and move slowly with no sudden movements. You can go nude or wear orange and if you follow some basic rules you'll get as close as you need to wildlife. Sure, camouflage helps but keep it in perspective.

Tracking. I've spent the better part of my life in the woods. I've trapped for several years semi-professionally. Identifying a track, knowing which direction it's heading and maybe how long ago *might* have some bearing on when and how to go about catching that animal (for food and clothes, tools, et al). Lots of undue emphasis placed here. In this day there just ain't too many injuns lookin' fer your scalp!

Music and storytelling. Much past experience has shown us that as a general rule, the more fluting, drumming, chanting and storytelling one is involved in,

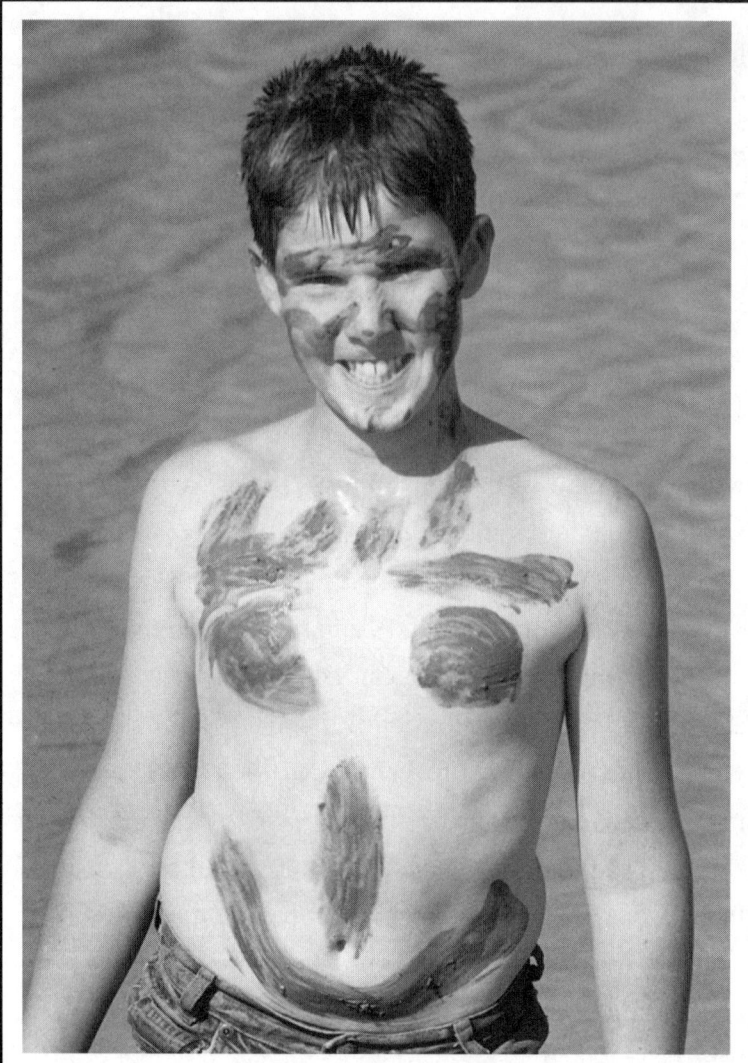

Camouflage, like tracking, can be fun and sometimes useful in a primitive lifestyle ... just keep it in perspective.

the less one knows about the actual (abstract) living *skills*.

Art vs. function. My (John) whole life has pretty well been devoted to trying to grasp an understanding of primitive living. Just about every minute of the past ten or more years has been spent on the research and practice (& teaching) of primitive skills. Paint and beads might make things look pretty but they won't fill your belly.

Chapter 7

"Naked into the Wilderness",
doing it, day 1

*T*his chapter is the first of three illustrating an actual, put to the test doing of the skills that we are always stressing: fire, cordage, traps, tools and shelters. We're also going to add containers to this list. You'll see by the photo's that our trip "Naked into the Wilderness" doesn't actually take us *naked*, but playing by the rules that *we* set we can't use the clothes that we're wearing for anything but just that - clothes (which are, in effect, a form of shelter). In reality where this limits us is "no pockets" (containers).

Geri and I are including in this series our young friend Ivan Anderson, whom you met earlier.

The day that we picked to photograph this chapter was a beautiful Saturday in early October - Indian summer here in the flint hills of western north-eastern Kansas (huh?). The days just prior to our outing were wet with just a bit of accumulation of rain. This

Indian summer in the Flinthills of Kansas.

particular Saturday morning we scraped ice from the windshield on our way to pick up Ivan. Things were damp ... but the sky was blue and the day heated to a too uncomfortably warm 70 + degree's by mid-afternoon.

Anytime that one, or as in this case three, head "Naked into the Wilderness", there will be a certain period at the beginning that needs be referred to as survival. This is when you first find yourself out there with absolutely nothing. In the case that we are illustrating for you here you need to be aware that we had many things going for us that just might not always be. Knowledge and experience of course is number one. Number two is the fact that this particular area of the United States is unusually rich in absolutely everything that one needs to live completely primitive - our resources are unlimited. Everything that one needs to head naked to the woods is literally within 200 yards of our dwelling. Add to this that we are aware just where to look for most of these resources and the trip begins to get kinda simple. On top of all this, we had flooding a coupla years back that left us with piles of drift which added to the ease of locating concentrations of shelter building materials.

Now that I've gone and taken the glory outta what we did, lets get to it.

•

• Day one •

I've told you just how easy that we had it, now let me now explain some of our drawbacks on day one. Ideally we would have begun right at daybreak to get the very most out of the daylight hours. This time of the year it is light enough to do something at 7 AM and will stay that way for about twelve hours. Three trained people can get a whole lot done in twelve hours - especially when looked upon as survival. But, we had also promised part of this day to help another local lad

13 year old Derick Hargrave.
Proud of the buckskin jacket he
made from scratch by himself.
Four skins were required.

get started on brain tanning his first ever deer skin (13 year old Der1ck Hargrave, who had helped on the canoe three days this season but was also committed to helping his dad farm. He has since turned four skins he tanned into a jacket).

Well, Geri worked with Derek until he got his initial steps completed while Ivan and I just kinda hung out. As before mentioned, we did need a container. We have developed a pretty simple method of putting together a truely functional basket with a minimum of hassle and so I got Ivan to work on this, a first time

The two components of this basket are fibers for cordage (L) and pliable twigs (below).

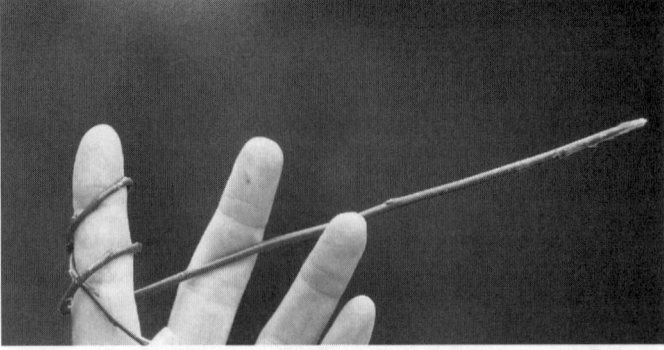

(Above) A hank of cord and a bunch of pliable shoots. (L & below) Lashing of the ends so simplifies the beginning that even I can do it.

(Right) The weaving in of the starters now becomes a simple matter.

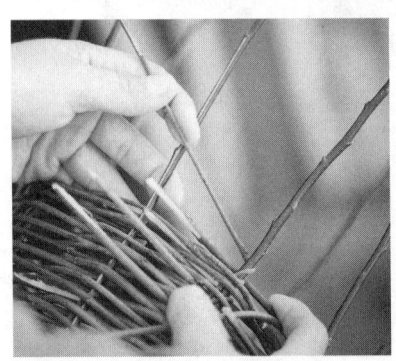

*Ivan builds (top), splicing in
(middle L) and finishing the
top (middle R). At this point
the finished basket is kinda
rugged (R).*

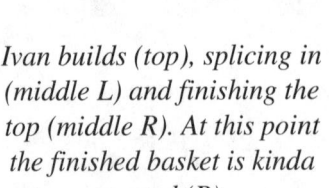

Using a stone blade, Ivan cuts off the scraggly ends (top). Left on the outside they would continually be snagging on brush. Left on the inside, they would take up room. Finished basket (R).

Ivan heads on his way to begin gathering. A length of cord would have allowed him to free his hand from carrying - don't know why he didn't think of that.

project for him so it took a bit longer than usual. By the time Geri was free and we were ready to head to the wilds, it was almost 1230 and we had a basket.

When we headed out we didn't have any blue-print of what we were actually gonna do or where we were going to head. We were just wingin' it, so to speak. We had a basket and the intentions of gathering (whatever), building a shelter, making a fire and setting out some traps.

Anytime that we head out like this, fire is the number one priority. The more you need it, the harder it is to get one. And there just are times that even under ideal conditions we don't get one. So, we place fire at the top of the list ... followed in short order by shelter. Sometimes when the weather is right (wrong?), shelter equals fire in importance because you might need a sheltered place in which to successfully make the fire. Today was sunny, warming, no threat of rain apparent. The past several days had been wet - so, we figured that while we worked on our house, the fire making materi-als would be best if left in the sun to dry as much as possible. Before the dampness of evening set in we would get serious about fire.

We gather. On the hillside as we approach the timber we find a few blocks of chert and knock off enough flakes to give us a supply of knives. These and a coupla extra good blocks are placed in the basket.

Material for fire is top in our minds - the three

of us search through the piles of drift we are working our way through, choosing, selecting, discarding. Between us, we end with a good selection of materials for drills, fireboards, tinder and fine kindling.

As the basket fills, Geri gathers some plant fibers (still-green dogbane) and makes up a length of cord to tie some of our "sticks" in a bundle. *Cord, another container.* We will also be needing a bit of fibers for traps and possibly in building so we gather what we can as we come across it. Our thinking is get it while we can. We can always leave it but we just might have a heck of a time finding it again. Find it, keep it ... you can stash it if you have to.

We have begun working through an oak grove and Ivan notices some acorns here and there - but all with worm holes ... left behinds by the squirrels. Lotsa acorn caps lying around. *(Tip: the larger acorn caps will make do for a bearing block when utilizing a bow drill.)* Now we don't stress a lot on plant foods but as I said, get it when you can. And acorns are no mistaking for something poisonous and are almost as magic a food as potatoes; carbohydrates, protein and fats. But we've been beat by the squirrels here. We did find walnuts though. So we gather some off the ground, green tho they might be, and figure something to chew on as well as bait. A bush of rose hips is also stripped, more for bait than food, but a good source of vitamin C.

We leave the oak grove and break out into

215

brightness and warmth of a sunny meadow. The drift-
wood line continues thru here, we appreciate the
warmth, find some more fibrous plants handy and
decide that this would be as good a spot for a house as
we might find. In a real situation I would have built in a
slightly different location but I opt for the openness
giving me easier and better photographs of the building.
My only other change in "reality" would be to snuggle
it in tighter to the timber to use it as a windbreak, but
also keeping in mind enough openness for sunshine.
Remember, winter approaches ... and we're naked. Our
only nearby water source, a spring, is about a quarter
mile off ... something to keep in mind in our later days
when it gets to be too much of a pain to walk that far
any time we need water. We'll worry about water
containers later.

*Spread in the sun to dry is a variety of fire making materials
along with walnuts, rose hips and plant fibers*

We spread our goodies out on a sunny log and take inventory. Plenty enough fibers and more nearby. Baits for traps. Stone blades and extra blocks of chert to make more. Most importantly, a good selection of pretty dry fire making materials.

Shelter time. The site selected is on a slight rise which will divert water in heavy rains. We've got a good location to collect sunlight for the major portion of the upcoming winter days. We're within touching distance of all the wood we will need for any framework and the meadow is loaded with enough weeds for a waterproof covering. Any leaves and other forest debutage is only about 100 yards off. These are the main reasons that we don't build closer to the water source. Another is that the roots of the stump out of which the spring runs has been host to denning snakes in years past.

We decide on the simplest of semi-permanent shelters, a wickiup based on a tripod. This shelter has been in use world wide since man has been around. We spend some time searching for just the right three sticks to make up the base ... this will support the entire works so it needs to be done well. We end with three about 10-12 feet long. Solid, not rotten. One has a "Y" at the small end into which the others fit snugly. We work it around until it's solid and can support our weight while hanging from it. There will be a lot of weight on it before we're done with it. We then pull all weeds and

The frame for the house is critical - it must support lotsa weight thru all weather. Here we set up a tripod that locks solidly (L). We then add a room for to sleep in off to one side (middle) and cover the whole with sticks (bottom).

By the time the day ends,
we have a pretty weatherproof
house
with sleeping arrangements

taller material from the inside of the "circle" it will eventually form to begin cleaning up the floor.

Since we've placed ourselves out here with no bedding, we build what many refer to as a debris hut off to one side as a bedroom. This is simply another long strong pole which is fitted onto and into the main house ... sort of an add-on room, but much less high. The pole where it attaches to the house is right at three feet high and the other end is placed on a coupla larger logs to get it about two and a half feet off the ground ... and is made secure however ... in our case by placing larger, heavier logs against it from the sides. Poles, limbs, branches, bark, et al will be placed leaning against this room to enclose it when it will then be completely filled with leaves, weeds, grasses and whatever forest and field debutage we can find that will act as an insulating material. Geri elects to work on this portion while Ivan & I work on the main room.

Us guys begin laying more and more sticks around the framework until there are not too many gaps left. Ivan comes up with the outside portion of a rotted cottonwood log (why do they rot from the inside out?) and we lay this over the larger gaps (Geri steals from us when we're not looking). As we all finish up with this initial covering of sticks, the real work lies ahead. The entire outside of the shelter has to be covered to a goodly depth with smaller diameter weeds & grasses - this will be what makes the simple sunshade/windbreak waterproof and into a "real" house.

Just a little "how-to" info here. The thicker diameter the weed and/or stick, the deeper must be the layer. Smaller diameter grasses will shed water much better with less depth.

The steeper the pitch of the roof, the less depth required.

Walls need not be as concerned with water penetration. Water wants to fall "down". Regardless of the angle that the wind might drive it, once it makes contact with your house, it begins to head "down". Our sheathing of poles - sticks - weeds - grasses is what prevents it from falling down into our house.

The more contact points that the water has to hit on its downward journey combined with the angle of the outside (in our case walls and roof are one) is what determines how dry you remain inside (we are not working with solid sheathing as in modern housing).

Imagine laying four to six inch diameter poles at an angle similar to our house side by side. Then lay another layer on top of that one. Ten feet long. Remember, we're not working with perfectly milled Lincoln Logs here and there will be many, many, many (can't stress that many, enough) gaps. Air spaces so to speak. Now pour five gallons of water at the top of the incline and watch how much comes inside how fast. It don't take much imagination to see that all but what the wood will absorb will be inside before making it to the bottom of

221

the ten foot incline. And as the wood absorbs to its saturation point, it all will come in. And this will be a roof/wall eight to twelve inches thick. Now make the same comparison with long grasses piled to a depth of, lets say, four inches thick. As an individual drop hits, it will ride the slope but always run around the stem until it falls again - how far depending upon the pitch. Every time it hits another blade, it stops its downward journey to run down the slope - then repeats, and repeats. The more stems, the longer it will slope (the ten foot ride) before it finally falls "down". By then, if you've got the proper depth, the water will be beyond the roof and over the walls to fall outside of the dwelling. The grasses, etc. should be placed on upside down so that the water will run down the branches/leaves instead of hitting more contact points sooner.

Whew!

So now, we got to gather weeds, stems and grasses. Lots! The smaller, the better. The entire outside of the house needs to be covered the deepest we can manage, layering from the bottom, up. This *shingling* effect will keep the water running on the outside. For the first night with little or no threat of rain we don't need to overworry ... *but!*

As we work on this we decide to leave a goodly portion of the East side open for ease of photographing ... then we eventually decide to enclose the upper portion of this and leave the bottom open permanently, making mats at a later date to close it up ... building a windbreak four or so feet high to protect this opening from the wind. The windbreak we'll place about three to five feet in front of and slightly encircling the house.

We'll be using fire inside of this home. Smoke will rise ... if no wind disturbs it. It's about impossible to make this type of primitive dwelling airtight. Watertight, yes. Airtight, no. The rising smoke will exit out of all of those tiny (hopefully) air spaces which water (hopefully) won't. (The hopefully's are in jest - this does work!) On top of all this smaller stuff, more large, heavy poles are placed to keep the lighter materials from blowing away.

Home fini.

Now fire.

Fire is *the* priority for us when we travel afield primitive. It's actually really a responsibility. Remember always that the more you need the fire, the harder it will be to produce. All other primitive skills are nothing more than mechanics. The finest bows and stone blades are nothing more than following rules and applying mechanics, even under primitive wilderness conditions. Not so fire. *(We are acquainted with a coupla individuals who could just about rub bricks and make fire but they are the exception, not the rule.)* Do everything right and you will not be guaranteed fire. This is the skill that should be practiced the most until you have learned to produce that all important coal under the

223

Ivan holds the fire board (top) and the flake used to make the notch. Then the mullein stalk is cut to length (R). A piece of root is carved and inserted into this (bottom L & R).

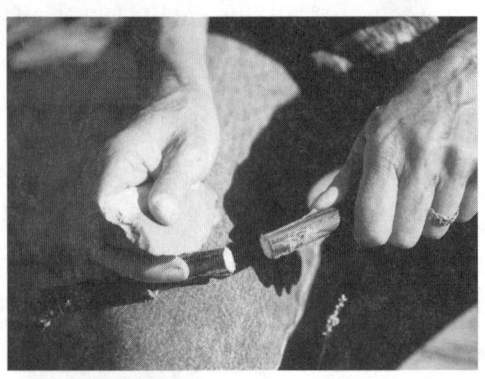

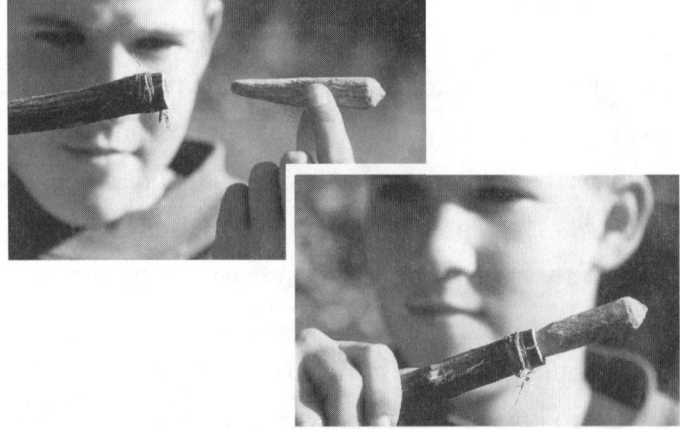

Geri and Ivan team up to make the coal (L) which Geri then blows to flame (middle). Then a break is taken to get the fire established (bottom).

severest of conditions. Enough, lets do it.

There are several techniques to produce fire primitively. I'll touch on here only the most common; bow drill and hand drill (both of these techniques are explained in depth in chapter two of NW-1).

What both of these methods have in common is a wooden drill spinning on another piece of wood we refer to as the hearth. The hand drill requires only two main components, the drill and the hearth. With the bow drill we have three other components to add; a bow, a bearing block and cordage ... the bow being the only *easy* part to come up with primitively.

The hand drill can work under pretty damp conditions by an experienced person, especially true if there is one or more along to help - with the bonus of having to come up with only two components. Under wet conditions it can be impossible unless you are very skilled and very lucky. When wet, we go with the bow drill. *(Tip: when using bow drill primitively make two strings ... use one to begin the hole and the other to actually make the fire. Primitive cord has this terrible habit of breaking just when you are at the point of getting that coal.)*

Today being only damp when we began and with good sun to dry and warm things up, we elect to use the hand drill. We have access to a variety of good drill materials available ... we decide to use a mullein stalk which is yet slightly green with an insert tip of cottonwood root just to give you another method of coming up with a straight drill of sufficient length when someday you may not have a good variety to choose from.

The mullein is cut at the bottom by scoring all around with a sharp blade and then just "popping" it off. The top (small end) can just be broken off. We carved the root piece down so that the exposed end would be a *slightly pointed blunt* and the other we *sharply pointed* (see photo's). A short length of cord was made from the dogbane (a strip of pliable bark, etc. would do as well) and we tied that securely around the base of the stalk where the tip would be inserted to prevent the stalk from splitting, and inserted the tip, rotating it and removing material when necessary so that the tip finally was seated securely - and straight. Other pithy stalks, rivercane, reeds, etc. can be used in this manner. The advantage of knowing methods such as this is that if only short, small pieces of quality drill material can be found, a hand drill can still be used. This cane trick was shown to us by Jim Dina of Connecticut several years back.

When we gathered the fire making materials, we picked up several different drill and hearth pieces so that we would have a variety to choose from if any one combination didn't work out. For the most part we found cottonwood limbs for the hearth. Now, cottonwood on cottonwood works, and works well, but is a bit more difficult than using a different, softer piece in combination. We also found root stock that would suffice. Past experience has shown us that soft on soft works best - but this is best when soft of two different stock are combined; yucca on cottonwood, mullein or sunflower on sycamore, etc. Still believing that softest on softest works best (not always so) I elected to go with root on root. It seems to me that when the two parts are too close in consistency, the right friction ain't there. It held true here. We had trouble creating just the right friction while starting the hole prior to cutting the notch - but I felt that by adding something in the hole to help roughen things up (fine sand, or in this case crushed and ground walnut shell), we could get it.

Actually it's best to find the best friction by experimenting with your various combinations first - before you get too pooped on the wrong one and have to wait a spell to try again. Though I knew we would have to work a bit harder with this choice I felt sure that we could make it work with three in tandem - and it did. We sure did have to work for it but by the time that we got it we had a coal so big that we coulda waited a week before blowing it into flame. But got it we did.

Traps. I've played some with traps over the years - it can be fun experimenting with various ar-rangements. I even at one time re-invented a trigger system (illustrated in our first book) - triggers that had been found in caves by the hundreds in the southwest -

Once we have fire we make up several trap sets (L) and set them out. Ivan checks one out up close (below).

but they couldn't figure out how they worked. What I'm gonna illustrate here is a simple modification of the famous Piaute deadfall.

Traps will make food for you while you do nothing. You expend the minimum of efforts for the greater return. Now, gathering of plants is alright, in fact we did some here today - but - your body requires a certain amount of elements and if you're gonna try to be a vegetarian on a long term basis anyplace but in the tropics, you're gonna die. Use plants as a supplement - an all important one - but rely on meat to stay alive.

229

The modified paiute that we have come up with takes only minutes to make - including the piece of cordage required. Takes about as long to set. **(Re-read chapter one on the dangers of hantavirus.)** Rodents are everywhere - set the trap in a meadow/in your house/in the woodpile/in the forest/by the water source/ in the mountains, forest, desert, arctic - just about anywhere and you'll get meat . And you don't have to expend hardly any energy at all ... just take it in. This day we made and set five traps each - (taking them down as we're not doing this for real this time). When we get around to day two we'll probably get well over 100 sets out.

This about takes care of day one. Three of us as a team have gone from nothing to fire/shelter/traps/ tools/cordage in about five hours. The evening around the fire before sleep will be spent in preparing cordage for traps and fire sets for tomorrow.

Chapter
8

"Naked into the Wilderness",
doing it, day 2

Day two ... *is a real-time montage of several days.*

We awake at first light. Geri tries to coax a coal from last evenings fire with no success and so she and Ivan team up to spin another into life. In a primitive survival situation, the first fire is the hard one. Once you get the initial one, the smart move is to prepare fire sets for the future. Yesterday we had taken several drills and hearths, dried them by the fire and experimented with each to find the easiest friction combinations, paired them, wrapped them in dried fluffy cedar bark for tinder, added a goodly handful of tiny, dry twigs and weed stems, stuck in a coupla stone blades, wrapped all

Preparing for a rainy day - fire boards, drill, tinder, kindling and flake knives - dry and ready ...

... ready for the elements in a protective covering of tightly packed dried grasses (top) and a final coat of barks (bottom).

this in dried grass, wrapped all this in dried layers of cedar bark and placed this bundle under a capping of a rounded half log with the middle rotted out. The resulting bundle will survive quite a wetting. We made three bundles like this and had other loose materials tied above the fire. It was this latter that we used for this mornings fire as the night was dry. We'll save the bundles for emergencies. (*We used one of these bundles not too long after. Our first snow of the season and 10° temperatures found Ivan and I out for the night. The interior of the house had been sifted with snow. It was dark, cold and we wanted a fire the first time so we used one of the bundles. It all worked perfectly.*)

So, fire. The first responsibility. Once you get the first one, you should have no trouble getting future ones ... *if you prepare.* Once a fire pit has had more than just a few hours fire, especially burning hard woods, coals will be there in the morning. If a hard drivin', goose drownin' storm hits while you're away and drowns your fire pit, you'll still have a bundle to fall back on.

While fire is being made and the house warmed, I head to check the traps. We got out ten the night before - four had critters, three small (mice) and one larger (packrat).

Note again here - **BEWARE OF HANTAVIRUS** *- this is a very real danger - refer to chapter one.*

The survival aspect of the initial wilderness contact is over - *fire* and *shelter*. Our goal is for a complete long term primitive living situation/camp. We have a water source nearby. One can go for an extended period with no food (of which we already have some).

As we awaken and loosen, both mentally and

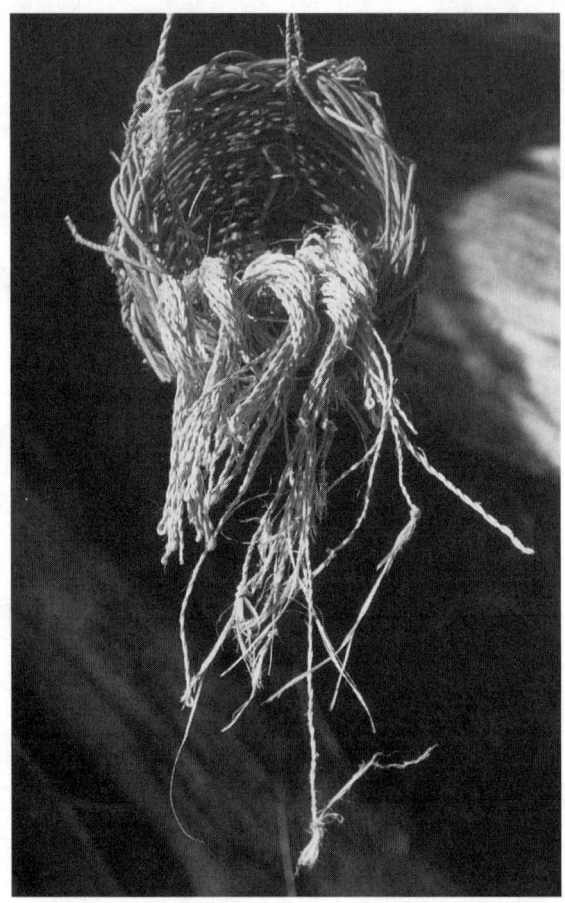

Several hanks of trap cords made beforehand (above) make it much speedier to make and set them when afield (below).

physically, we warm ourselves around the fire, eat what we have and make more lengths of cord for traps. Our first project of the day will be to collectively set out more traps - they can be supplying us with nourishment as well as clothing material while we while the hours away at whatever. Within just two and a half hours of waking we have a total of 70 traps set - all within a few

Planning again for bad days ahead we spend time preserving, by drying, some of our catch.

hundred yards walk from our home. Rodents work during the daylight hours as well as during the night and we plan to capitalize on this.

Since we are supposed to be naked, we need think of clothing. An extended cold weather storm could be uncomfortable at best, quite likely fatal.

A blanket can be woven with not too much

difficulty from rodent skins, of which we'll have several soon. Woven rabbit skin blankets were/are considered **the** warmest cold weather garment by some of the Canadian Indian tribes and early white explorers. We like to think big - deer - so I'll spend much of my day working on this. Gettin' one will be the easy part, dressing it into buckskin will be another days project - especially leaving the hair on for winter.

A really functional blanket/cape/robe can be made from grasses, cattail leaves or tules. Inspiration #1 for this comes from the Iceman found in the Italian Alps with one several years back (he was *found* several years back - he was *using it* about 5,300 years back). #2 inspiration comes from seeing the one made by Bart Blankenship of Boulder, Colorado from tules - he tested it for several hours in the rain - dry! So for our immediate future, clothing. I'll prepare to get Bambi - Ivan & Geri can work on a grass outfit.

Geri grabs some of the longer chert blades and cuts a coupla armloads of taller slough grass (dead & dried at this time of the year) and then soaks the big ends to make them pliable. Ivan gathers bunches of velvet leaf, strips them clean of leaves and stems and hauls bundles of the stalks back to camp - for cordage and also for layering on the shelter for further waterproofing. Some 40 to 50 feet of cord will be required to tie the grass garment (coat?) together. Ivan makes several lengths of about six feet. After less than an hour

Long slough grass is twined together into mats (top). The three finished pieces (middle), one for the back and two for the front, after being tied together are cut to even lengths by chopping with an ax (bottom).

*Geri looking dangerously beautiful in her grass
outfit with ax and wilderness dog.*

of soaking Geri and Ivan begin to twine small handfuls of the grass together.

They make one mat about three feet wide at the top (large, or bottom end of the grass), which will taper in as the grass thins towards the bottom of the garment. Placing the bottom of the grass up will allow the water to run *off* leaf joints and not cause it to drip *in* to you. The taper could be compensated for but we're in more of a need of function than art at the moment so we don't spend the extra time on it. Two more mats are made, each slightly wider than one half of the first. The large mat makes the back, the two others the front. They are twined twice for extra strength at the top (bottom of grass stem) which is folded over (reason for soaking). As the grass dries, it will shrink and the ties here will have to be re-tightened. At two other places the grass is twined together about six or eight inches below each other. The two are tied loosely at the shoulders to the back and a bundle of shorter grass is tied over the gap left. A tie is made about 18 inches down at each side to allow ample room to slip the arms in and out. Geri steps into it and two ties are added to close the front. This would be terribly uncomfortable on bare skin - but it would provide shelter - insulating *in* some warmth, keeping *out* most rain and wind. Talk about roughin' it. When in the house it can be used as a door. Smaller, thicker versions of the mats are made for sandals.

I sit and fashion a coupla ax heads from the

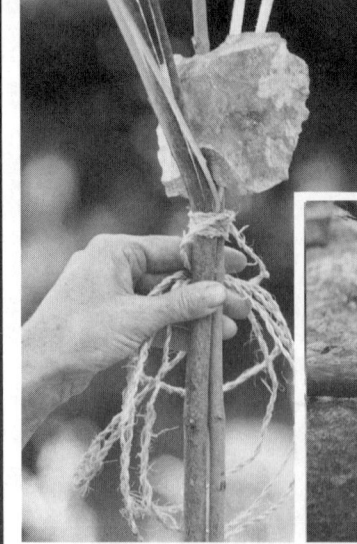

Several small diameter, pliable basket type shoots are individually wrapped and tied off (top L&R). One or two larger diameter pliable shoots, such as arrow shafts, are split, wrapped and tied off.

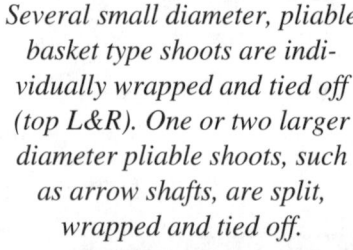

pieces of chert we had gathered yesterday, using a fist sized hammerstone of firm limestone - things work well and this takes only 30-40 minutes. These could be used hand held but much more efficiency is gained if they are hafted to some sort of handle. I've come up with a coupla quickie methods to do this and I employ them here. Once materials are gathered this project takes only 15 - 20 minutes per ax making a total time per hafted ax from beginning, including the making of the stone head, of just over 30 minutes. Others more proficient at knapping could cut this time somewhat. (Note photos for these techniques.)

While I roam gathering hafting sticks I head off to the cordage patch and bundle me up a goodly

Taking advantage of a wonderful Indian summer afternoon, I head to the spring, strip fibers and make a length of cordage ...

... which I use to bundle up a bunch of fibrous stalks to haul back to the house (top) from which I make a 15 foot length of six ply cord (L). Leftover stalks are placed on the house as additional covering.

armload of stalks - using the freshly stripped fibers to tie them up. Since leg rolling cordage is made simpler by dampening the fibers and the day is sunny and warm, I decide to sit by the spring and make up several feet of two ply cord. By the time I run out of the small-ish bundle that I took to the spring I have about 50 feet made - which is just about the right amount that I'll need for one of my next projects, a deer snare.

•

The two methods that I'm going to <u>kinda</u> illustrate the taking of large game with here are strictly <u>illegal</u>. What I'll do here is take the time to manufacture the items that are necessary - I will not illustrate any actual setting of these. As far as I know, snaring of deer is illegal anywhere. The other method I'll refer to, the cross bow trap, is not only illegal but is also a man killer so it should be strictly off limits. I'll show no methods of setting these. No triggers. These traps, among others, are methods that were employed at one time in the past to stay alive. <u>What was acceptable at one time is no longer.</u>

•

I head back to camp with a bundle of fibrous stalks on my shoulder - small sticks for hafting and several pieces of chert tucked inside. Once there I make up several short lengths of cordage, then haft the two axes. I take the 50' length of two ply cord that I had made at the spring, divide it into thirds, tie one end together and cut what is now a loop to give me three equal lengths - these I roll in the reverse direction of how I made the first to give me a 15-16 foot length of six ply cord. This heavier rope I will double over in such a way as to make a deer snare. This latest maneuver takes only 10-15 minutes. I note that Geri and Ivan are about an hour from being done with their grass cape project and so I grab my axes and head out to find suitable material for a bow.

To make a quickie, fully functional hunting bow is simple - *if* you have the right materials at hand. The tools mean nothing if there isn't the proper wood available - and by proper wood I mean not just good bow making woods. Hickory, ash and several other woods make for real fine bows - if the wood is dried under ideal conditions. These ideal conditions don't exist naturally in the wilds.

The best of bow woods used green will give a sorry, sappy bow - too much moisture in the wood makes for ample bending but the wood don't snap back enough to make for good shooting. Here I refer to bows capable of killing deer sized game. The wood must be dried properly to give the best the wood has to offer. In the wilds, with bark usually left on, being wetted and then dried repeatedly, the wood most always rots. Rotted wood makes no bow. But, have heart. Certain woods, because of their rot resistance, will dry, if not perfectly, at least good enough to make a suitable bow. Osage orange is one. Eastern red cedar (really a juniper) and certain species of elm will work also (all of which are available here). The way we check just what will work and what won't (we hate to use names - much better to describe characteristics) is to find limbs that appear dead and when you bend them just seem to resist breaking and *snap* back when released..

Our old standby that we use regularly here is the lower limbs of the eastern red cedar. When this tree is crowded in dense growths, the bottom limbs die off. We look for straightish limbs with bark intact but with no live needles attached. Try to break one of these off and you'll understand just why they'll make such good bows.

For these quickie bows some simple rules. Maybe remove the bark if it's thick or if you have the time to spare. With these cedar limbs we can leave it on. It may crack and snap but it's only the bark, not the wood beneath (hopefully). If the bark is removed make sure that you don't cut into the outer growth ring beneath the surface - this keeps the back of the bow from tearing apart and you will want to keep this integrity intact. The limbs grow tillered - meaning that they get smaller in diameter the further out they go. Example: place the tips of any piece of even dimension lumber on a surface a coupla feet off the floor. Step in the middle and note where the wood does all of its bending - and where it eventually will break ... at the middle. To make this piece bend evenly overall so as not to break at the middle you need remove wood from the top (the inside of the curve or the belly of the bow. The back, or outside, is trying to tear apart. One solid growth ring running from tip to tip helps to prevent

Geri holds two dead'ish cedar limbs (L) that are tied together at the large ends (middle) to make a fully functional bow (bottom).

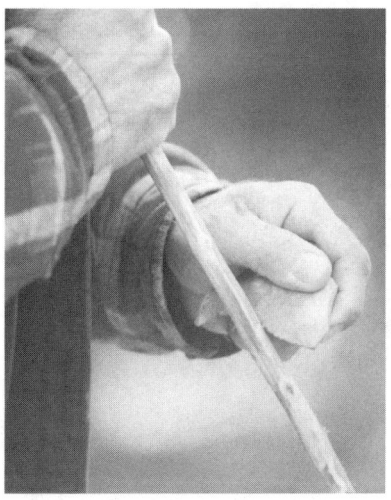

A cedar shaft is smoothed (above) and notched (R).

The other end is split (L) and a point is hafted (below).

The finished bow is more than powerful enough to propel the dart into a deer sized animal.

*this. The piece will be **thicker at the middle than at the tips**. You can remove wood from the sides but this matters much less in the tillering (distributing the bend evenly). As expected, wood removed from the sides corresponds mathematically at 50%. Want to take away 50% of the draw weight, remove 50% of the width. Removing from the thickness is a bit more delicate as the factor here is times (x) 8. A little bit goes a long way. So, almost all tillering is done from the belly of the bow. Slowly.*

Look at the photos. I found two almost identical limbs - each *grown* tillered. I bound them together at

The house and compound at end of day 2.

the mid section and I've got a finished bow. The draw
weight is limited by the thickness *or* length of the
limbs. It does not bend at the middle (double thickness)
but does so evenly from either side out to the tips. (The
initial inspiration for this simple idea comes from Tim
Baker.)

So, where are we at. Sometime after mid day.
We've got our second fire going, eaten a little from
traps set out yesterday and put out about 60 more. Geri
and Ivan have finished one grass outfit. I spent the
morning working on approaches to obtaining large
game ... not really for the meat as the small traps will
more than suffice to feed us ... but looking ahead to the
necessity of clothing (besides everything else provided). Geri thinks of the deer as K-Mart. Every time
any of us walks by the house another armload of weeds
or grass is laid on for water and wind proofing.
The wind has been a real danger with our fire so
I begin work on the wall of logs and branches from the
drift to form a compound outside the door of the house.
This will not only protect the fire in the house but will
also give us a protected outside work area with fire.
Geri and Ivan make a mid-day trap run and return with
several various rodents, a few we eat now. Splitting
open, spreading with sticks and drying in the sun
preserves the rest for a rainy day. The skins are dried
for future use (probably a blanket would be #1 but there

are many uses for rawhide).

We have a few hours of daylight left so Geri and Ivan begin the making and setting out of even more traps. As long as we are able to preserve the meat, we'll keep collecting for those days when we might not be able to get around for some reason - and the need for the skins is immediate. I spend the afternoon working down a straight limb of cedar into an arrow/dart to work with the bow. Tho simple it still took me a coupla hours to put it all together. Then I needed to place both the bow and snare out which would have taken a certain amount of time.

Chapter
9

"Naked into the Wilderness",
Doing it,
day three, plus.

Ivan uses a hand held ax to chop down an oak tree for use as a digging stick.

*O*ne of the more basic tools that one finds themselves working with out primitively is really also the simplest ... the digging stick. From hour one of day one we all had stout walking sticks. I initially got mine to aid these cracklin' old knees and worn-out back but it is actually a multipurpose stick. It was used to prod, probe and turn over things. It was, a digging stick. Now lets do it right (if there is such a thing).

Ivan and I head to the timber looking for suitable sticks. Geri stays to home to help Derick smoke the four deer skins that he just finished for a jacket. It takes us almost an hour of searching to find three of what we consider fine ones. Two are dead, one is a live, standing, inch and a half diameter oak which we elect to sacrifice for this learning experience. One dead piece, of oak, is plenty long and will need be shortened. Another is of cedar about the right length. The third, the live oak, we cut down with a hand held stone ax that

After some little searching (its not always easy to find quality digging sticks), we end with three that will work.

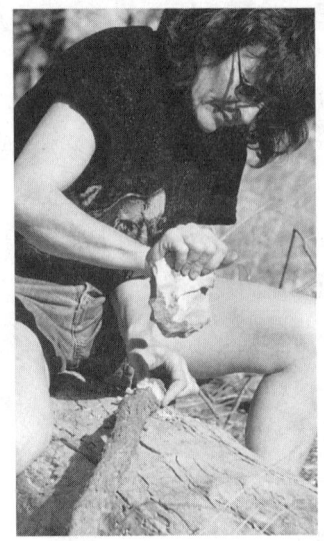

Geri uses the ax to cut the oak to length (upper L) while she and Ivan work at the fire to shape the tools (R).

We all three busy ourselves with our personal sticks (above). The final shaping takes place by scraping (below L) and sanding (below R).

The finished tools.

Ivan made this morning.

Heading back to camp we are joined by Geri and Derick, who tags along. Ivan rounds up hand drill fire making materials and he and I tag team to make short order of a coal. Geri gathers tinder and kindling and blows our coal to flame and we soon have a solid fire. Ivan decides to work with the longer of the dried pieces and his first task is to simply burn it off to the elected length. I use the fire to shape and harden the working end of the shorter cedar piece. Geri takes Ivan's hand ax and cuts the green oak to length. She could burn it but it's much faster to chop green wood.

When I speak of fire hardening the wood I'm simply referring to removing moisture from it. The dead pieces, tho dried, will yet retain a certain amount of moisture and while this might add strength to certain

257

woods that become more brittle when dried (e.g. cotton-wood), others such as oak will become stronger as it is dried further. We use the fire carefully ... we don't want scorched or charred. What we do here is begin to char and then scrape away anything that is loose and weak. We do this slowly, a little at a time so that we retain control. We try not to let the wood flame. As soon as it begins to, we take our stone blade and scrape away any of the char. It takes several minutes of this to shape the end. Two of the sticks we make pointed. The third, the cedar, I leave a bit wider of a point, almost a spade head. With this one I want to move a bit of dirt. With all of these we place the end tip off center ... that is, the point is not at the center of the wood. Many woods are pithy and/or have weak center growth rings. More strength is gained by placing the ends off center (from Peter Binden of Australia). The green oak that Geri is working is scorched back for about six inches. Scorch and scrape ... repeat. Again.

It really doesn't seem to take any longer for her to complete the point on the green piece as it does us working on the dried. When finished we end with three durable working sticks. The pointed ones, if longer, could well be used a spears.

We didn't need get quite so fancy. The reason we needed the sticks now was for to dig clay - our main purpose of the day. Though in a real life situation I would hope to be working a deer skin into clothing about now, our traps of the day before didn't pan out (no road kills). A major step up in our "living" camp is ceramics. "My kingdom for a pot" said Steve Watts once to me after a several day long primitive outing. A coupla small pieces of meat and maybe a handful of greens or tubers will satisfy much more when made into a soup. Two bites becomes a pint. So lets make up

Geri digs deep into a bank to get clean clay (top) and then she and Ivan add water to dampen it more (lower).

some kitchen ware.

Clay, treated properly, turns into ceramic. Ceramic you can store water in - and cook in. Above a certain temperature, clay (dirt of a sort) vitrifies - turns into something that won't fall apart in water. Kinda magic. (Primitive pottery is covered in detail in chapter eight of NW-1.) Well we got clay. Along a creek (pronounced crick) bank we have found several cuts exposing a greenish, sticky substance. Clay. We roll it

Temper is added (L) and pots are made (below).

into pencil sized coils and test it by wrapping around our fingers. Pliability is a must. We dig three trays (pieces of bark) full, dampen it (it's a bit dry) and carry it back to the camp. Tho we'll soon want to make up some water containers and larger community cooking pots, we now settle for individual all purpose cooking/ eating pots.

The clay needs to be cleaned some before using. There are too many impurities in it - mostly things that might explode when gotten hot. Tho there are many ways to do this, in situations like this we have found it most expedient to simply go thru it a pinch at a time, taking out any sticks and stones. Once we have a fist sized ball, we add a small handful of sand (this temper adds stability to the material as it heats and cools) and mix well. A lot of pounding and slapping to remove any and all air, add a little water if and when it seems dry and begin to form into a pot. It don't take long for us to have several drying. Tho Ivan seems to feel that this might be woman's work, he is reminded that the completely self-reliant person has to be competent in the entire circle of skills.

The pots now have to air dry for several days (depending on the climate). The purpose is to dry the product slowly. If moisture leaves too quickly, cracks are likely to appear. We seldom have troubles with this stage of drying - just leave it in a shady spot, maybe out of the wind. Geri has, in the past, force dried them by moving them carefully around a cooking fire. Ashes from the area ended up covering the pots (not intentionally) and she felt that this may have helped in absorbing moisture. Whatever, she built them Monday A.M. and fired them Wednesday A.M. This stuff shrinks when drying so make certain to go slow or the outside drying (shrinking) faster then the inside will create cracks. The more even the thickness of the walls & bottoms of pots, the more evenly they will expand and contract during the heating & cooling process of firing. The thinner the walls, the less variance in expansion/contraction when subjected to heat (either when firing or cooking). Therefore thinner is stronger.

Once air dried, it's time to really dry them - with fire.

Firing runs the clay thru two critical stages. The first is when the pots reach temperatures of around 212° - the boiling point of water. The remaining moisture leaving the walls of the pots (as steam) too fast will actually cause minor explosions sending spalls of hot clay flying - sometimes almost like a hand grenade. Heating slowly can help prevent this. We burn a lot of fuel at this stage to insure that we run from about 180° to 225° real slow! Once thru this first critical stage we move the fire closer to the pots, raising the temperature a little faster until about the 600° to 800° range when the clay goes thru its second critical stage, the loss of natural moisture (vitrification) - changing at this stage from clay to ceramic. If rain was to interrupt the firing below this second stage the clay would blow into pieces but it could be soaked and used again as clay. After vitrification it's clay no more. Then the only uses for the shards would be to grind/pound them into tiny bits to be used as temper.

The firing process that we have developed over several years of trial and error utilizes a tremendous

Ivan and I do another handdrill (L) and the pots are fired (below).

amount of wood but has given us the very best results with the fussy clay that we have available to us here. During the experimental stages that got us to where we are, the percentage of success with our firings ran anywhere from 0% to 60%. Most all primitive potters that we spoke with during our early learning stage were happy with a 50% success rate. We weren't. We now run a success rate of from 90% to 100% (we consider it a success if it does not spall, holds water and we can cook in it). Minor cracking, tho unattractive, oftentimes works.

We build a fire (size depending on the number of pots to fire) of small sized material - small because this will be spread into a circle into which the pots will be placed. Large limbs, etc. will not transfer well from this initial pile into a circle. Trying to build a circle fire initially is work ... lots of material, hustling and maybe kerosene a necessity. Best to build the pile fire, spread it and then add the longer limbs (small diameter at first) so as to have a complete circle of flames. Leave an opening at first which you can walk thru to place your pots with-in. Insure that the ground that you are firing on is dry - otherwise rising steam can crack the product. We place the pots on stable rocks (those which won't explode) or pot shards from past failures to better allow heat to surround them. On their sides or upside down works best for us. Move this fire closer and closer slowly. When we are certain the temperature has reached the second critical stage of 800° ± we build the walls of the fire higher than the pots themselves with substantial sized limbs and then lay a roof over the pots of more limbs. This insures that the fire heats more gradually than if we just pushed the flames directly onto the pots. Also by roofing it in this manner a draft is created, sucking air in from the sides and forcing it up thru the roof something akin to a draft furnace thereby (we think) finally subjecting the pots to a higher temperature. By the time that the roof falls in and coals come into direct contact with the pots, they are glowing.

Slow to heat, slow to cool. As the fire settles in we push the ashes and coals over the pots to insure slow cooling. If we fire in the early morning (less likely winds), it will be late afternoon or into evening before we uncover them. Firings in midday are usually left overnight. We have witnessed pots cracking in one's hands when taken out too soon. Be patient. We were, and we have three nice sized personal pots.

•

Clothing is still something that we have to bear in mind. The grass outfit, fashionable as it is, is uncomfortable to wear against bare skin. Kinda not the easiest to get around in either. We hope to have a deer to go thru (literally) at any time. We have several skins left from our trapping forays of the past coupla days and Geri comes up with the idea of instant moccasins.

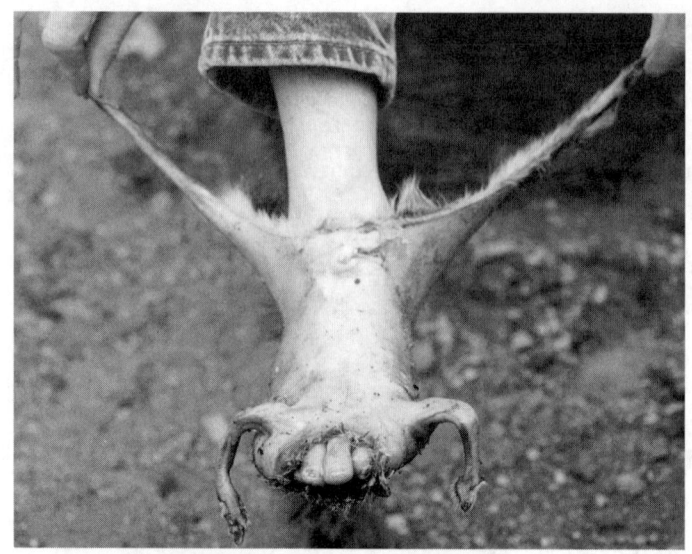

Squirrel skin pulled over foot (top), front end tied off (L) and two pair ready (below) ... to give a puppet show?

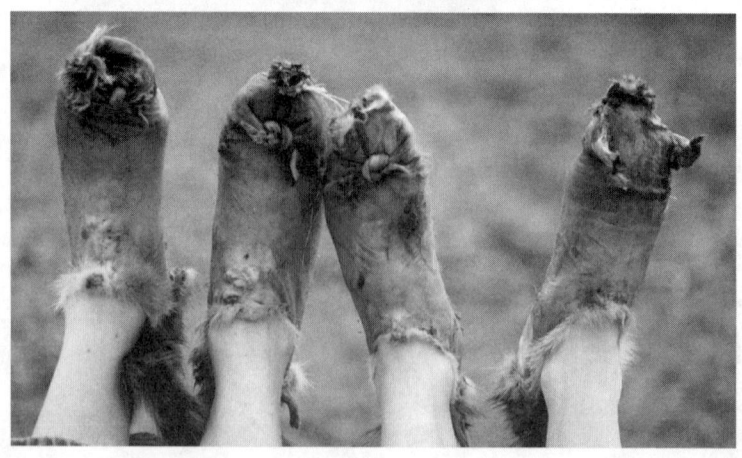

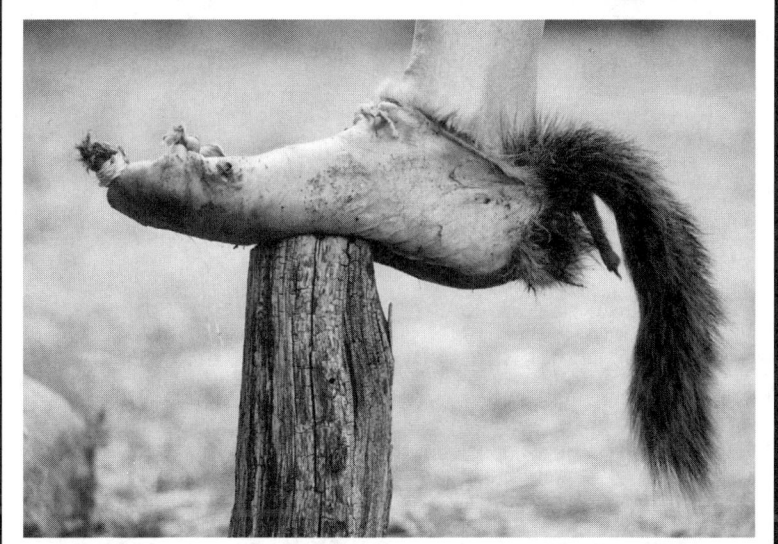

The final product makes for a pretty comfortable piece of footwear with next to nothing expended as far as time or effort.

When we skinned them out we case skinned them - that meaning that we just kinda slipped the skin from the back end to the nose, about like inverting a sock. To do this you need only open the rear end from one foot, down the leg thru the anus up to the other foot. If the tail is to be left on you need work around it a little to either pull the skin from it or simply cut it free at the base. We didn't skin over the heads (should have) but this opening can either be left for aeration of the toes or tied off if it's cool out there. The front legs if cut off will leave air holes (which could be tied shut). If left on leave them be if they don't get in the way. Otherwise you can simply tie them together. When the skin dries it will stay pretty much in place. The back legs are used to tie around the ankle to hold it in place on the foot. Do whatever you want with the tail. Geri wrapped hers around the ankle and tucked it in for additional warmth (and to keep from tripping on them). Ivan let his drag (to cover his tracks? ... joke).

These skins don't need to be treated in any way to work. You can simply wear them until they dry and they will shape to your foot and also stay somewhat flexible. If you take them off or simply don't move your feet as they are drying they will become stiff and uncomfortable. Better yet would be to rub the brain, kidneys, liver, fat, etc. into the raw pelt thereby adding oils which will actually kinda tan the pelt out - at least making it softer and more flexible. We here are illustrating using squirrel skins. Muskrats and other small furry critters would work as well. In cooler times, layering with an outer pelt of a larger animal such as a small possum or raccoon would add quite a bit of insulation/comfort. Leaving the hair out will add to your traction - leaving it in will give warmth.

Synopsis

Day one, the survival day. Weather cooperated. We got a good tight shelter with a sleeping bag arrangement built near a water source and made fire. Flint like rock was located and collected and several stone blades were made. Fibrous plants were found in abundance ... several traps were put out. We were up late making trap length cordage around the fire and preparing fire bundles.

Day two. We had to make another fire but had no trouble as we had dried and prepared materials the night before. Fire from this point on should be no problem as we'd have coals in the morning from a fire burning continuously besides having the security of prepared bundles. Some food was obtained from the traps and many more had been placed out, the final number for the day would exceed 100. The trap lines will vary locations regularly to avoid over trapping any one area. The biggest accomplishments and goals for this second day are in the area of obtaining clothing; the grass outfit and the two deer traps. Tightening up of the house and sleeping area is ongoing.

This second day is a real marathon workout for the three of us. *Over 400 feet of cordage has been made today alone!*

Day three is the beginning of a sustaining rather than "survival" period. The making of ceramics now places us in the living category. From this point on our time would be spent improving the homestead, working on animal skin clothing, preparing and storing foods for the coming months, making certain that there was an abundant supply of wood for the fire close by, creating several water containers, and ... well, you get the picture. Obtaining large game will be a boon for us but also time consuming as we will have to take care of the meat and skin(s).

A hunting bow will come along shortly for something to carry along on our excursions - not hunting trips as such but to be used as opportunity offers. There are lots of ways to better spend time than hunting - traps will do the "hunting" for us.

> *Primitive peoples, no matter the time period, were all born into a material culture of some sort. Their family and/or community provided the necessities of life even if it was as basic as fire, clothing and tools. Placed naked in the wilderness, it became survival for them too.*

Chapter
10
Storms

by Geri

*T*he trees that shed their leaves had been bare for two turnings of the moon yet the sun heated the days as if it were still the warm season. Each night a light frost coated every blade of grass with puffs of ice crystals and each morning the sun melted it away, leaving the land freshly washed.

The people of the Red Hills had chosen a snug, timbered place along a deep, flowing river as a place to wait out the cold season, but it seemed that the cold had chosen to go elsewhere. Each day was as bright as the one before, and the mood of the camp was light and almost carefree.

There was little need to dry meat from the animals that the hunters brought in. The women simply hung it in the shade and let the cool nights keep it fresh. The hunters complained some about the difficulty of moving quietly through the dry, crackling grass and leaves, but they managed to hunt well in spite of it. Even the old ones, with few teeth, grew fat.

Although his mate, Is Tall, was near to giving birth, Broken Jaw and two others set out to hunt a small herd of horses that had been spotted a few days before. Birthing was, after all, a woman's concern and nothing he could do anything about. And besides, horses had not been plentiful for many seasons. Just thinking about the sweet tasting, rich, red meat made him swallow the juices that collected in his mouth.

The men walked purposefully across the rolling

hills, covering as much distance as they could. Late in the afternoon, they stopped at a small spring and made camp. There was little conversation, as each man set about his tasks.

Beaver Tail drew a bundle out of his carrying bag and untied the cord that held it bound together. He lifted a split-out piece of root and examined the charred hole that was set slightly in from its edge and the wedge shaped notch that fanned out from the depression. He pushed the end of his finger into the shallow dip, and being satisfied with it, he picked up a length of plant stalk. He placed the flat piece of root on the ground, pushed a scrap of bark under the notch, and held it all firmly in place with his foot. He bent over the hearth piece, placed the stalk in the hole, and began to spin it between his palms. He spun the drill swiftly, and as his hands reached the bottom of the drill he quickly lifted first one hand then the other to the top of the drill, always keeping the tip pressed firmly into the hole, and spun downward again. Thick smoke billowed up from the friction of fiber to fiber as a pile of dark dust collected in the notch. Beaver Tail continued spinning until smoke poured forth from the pile. He set the drill aside, sat back on his heel and with a thin stick carefully separated the hearth from the pile of dust that began to glow. The pungent, welcome smoke tickled his nostrils causing him to rub his nose.

Broken Jaw took over, lifting the piece of bark

273

that held the glowing coal and placed it in the handful of shredded bark he had prepared. He lifted the tinder bundle and waved it back and forth slowly. His hand appeared to be but a cloud of smoke as the tiny coal began to feed on the tender fuel. He brought the smoking hand to his mouth and blew long steady puffs into the tangle of bark. Quickly, it flamed up and he lowered it to the ground, gently criss-crossing small twigs on top of it. As the fire consumed itself, he added thicker pieces of wood until he could leave it to burn without constantly nurturing it.

Beaver Tail shrugged off the large deerskin that he wore tied over his shoulders, and nodded at Broken Jaw as he sliced thick pieces off the chunk of elk meat that He Walks had carried in his bag.

He Walks had tied a long branch horizontally between two small trees that grew in front of the place chosen for the fire. Against the support he began laying up a sloped back with branches and grass. While Beaver Tail scraped out coals from the fire and skewered the meat over them, Broken Jaw helped finish the lean-to, laying more grass over the back.

The sky was clear as darkness chased the sun into hiding. The three hunters sat at the entrance of the shelter they had hastily put up and ate the elk meat. Its juices ran down their arms as they lifted it to their mouths, and they wiped the wetness on the deerskin tunics that covered their chests.

A mere promise of morning tinted the eastern horizon when they stirred, waken by the pressure of the water they had drank the night before. Broken Jaw and He Walks shook frost off the deerskins they had covered themselves with, folded them, and laid them in the back of the shelter. Beaver Tail tied his across his shoulders which was his habit, and without speaking they all shouldered their carrying bags, picked up their weapons, and started off.

It grew still as morning gained control, so that it seemed the men were the only living creatures in this land of red dirt and tall waving grasses. The hollows of the rolling hills took on deep shadows as the sun lifted itself from its slumber and brightly lit the day. The men walked northward and breathed an audible sigh when a slight warm breeze came up from the west and ruffled the reddish grass stems. They quickened their step and strained their eyes for signs of the valley they sought.

It wasn't long before they saw a hawk soaring in a high wide circle in front of them. It rode high, then suddenly dove down out of sight only to swoop up again, still soaring. It was clear that a dip in the land lay in front of them, and they approached it carefully.

As they got nearer they could see the opposite side of a small valley and they crawled on their bellys to look cautiously over the edge. Below them a herd of about twenty horses grazed quietly. A stout, dust-colored stallion lifted his head continuously, first

275

smelling the air for danger then for an inviting scent from one of his mares.

Without a word, the three men nodded to each other and drew back from the edge of the drop-off. Beaver Tail and He Walks set off toward the west, following the contour of the land. Broken Jaw slowly made his way to the eastern end of the valley and studied the terrain. He had hunted here before and knew that it was well situated for their plans. Both sides of the valley were steep, with sharp rock outcroppings and sheer rock faces. The only way in or out for the horses was at either end.

A tall thicket of sand plums choked the eastern end and Broken Jaw took refuge behind it and a large boulder that would keep him out of sight. He was in for a wait while the other two hunters worked their way to the opposite end. There the valley widened out so that it would take two men to keep the horses from turning back and escaping. Broken Jaw sighed, If the wind had come up from the east, he would have been the one to chase the horses into the spears of the two hunters. Now it was on him alone to bring down at least one of the creatures. Hidden as he was, he was able to move about freely as he carefully checked his two spears. They were as long as he was tall, thin and flexible. He pulled several foreshafts from the bag that hung from his waist, and laid them on the ground in front of him. He had done all of this the night before but now he did it again, feeling each sharp stone edge of his points. He had tested the foreshafts for their fit into the openings at the end of his spears, but he checked once more. Choosing two, he placed the rest back. He curled his fingers around the handle of his spear thrower and in turn seated each feathered spear end into its hook.

When he was satisfied with his weapons, he looked carefully around the boulder and watched the horses. The brightness of the sun had become muted as he prepared, and he glanced up, surprised at the gray clouds that now choked the sky.

He turned his attention back to the horses just in time to watch a chunky mare wheel suddenly and nip at her colt. In an instant the rest of the horses seemed to explode in a frenzy of rearing and kicking. Bewildered at the actions of their dames, foals squealed and nickered frantically. Broken Jaw wet his finger and held it in front of him, wondering if the wind had shifted slightly. It still held from the west, and seemed to increase its strength. The horses could not have caught his scent and it seemed too soon for the other two hunters to have gotten in place. Broken Jaw watched the frightened display in front of him and soon understood the horses' behavior.

He felt a sudden cold in the wind and watched a cloud-like line of snow begin to move swiftly across the valley much as a deerskin door flap falls across a shelter entrance. Soon he could no longer see the

277

willows at the other end of the valley ... or the horses. The wind drove the snow closer and he could feel the ground shake as the herd bolted and began to run past him. The large flakes blurred his vision and he could barely make out the individual horses as they scrambled by him bunched closely together. They seemed not to notice him as they crashed by with their tails tucked tightly against the wind.

Broken Jaw stood erect and threw his spear into the running mass. As suddenly as they had appeared they were gone. There had not been time enough to throw his second spear, even though he had gotten it seated into the thrower and lifted back over his shoulder. The cold wind was all he heard now. The ground no longer shook. Stepping from the relative shelter of the boulder and the brush, he felt the full force of the wind-driven snow push against his face, stinging his eyes. Bending with the wind he walked back and forth across the choppy path left by the hooves of the frightened horses. He looked for his spear, that should have bounced free of its foreshaft, if he had indeed hit one of them. Already snow began to fill and cover the tracks when he saw the dust-colored horse lying on its side. The stallion rolled its eyes with panic as Broken Jaw came nearer. The stone point of the foreshaft had cut into the horse's spine and now its powerful legs were useless. He could only lift his head and scream in defiance. The scream stopping in mid-flight as Broken

278

Jaw's knife sliced through the horse's airway on its way to the neck artery. The widely flared nostrils became narrow slits as an ear twitched one last time.

It was only then that Broken Jaw began to really feel the sudden cold that came with the snow. He turned to face the way he had come and could see nothing. The valley, and even the thicket with the shelter it offered, had disappeared. His eyelashes caught the snow and became fringes he could barely see through. The single-layered deerskin garment he wore did little to stop the bite of the cold as the wind pushed its way through and chilled his sweat. He shivered slightly and could feel his fingers stiffening as the cold brought pain that seeped under his fingernails.

A heaviness settled into the bottom of his belly as the realization of his situation became clearer to him. Was it not uncommon for careless hunters to die in storms such as this?

Blood from the severed artery darkened the ground in a widening pool and froze into red crystals. Survival for him now, he realized, lay in immediate action. With the snow swirling blindly around him Broken Jaw quickly slit into the belly of the horse with his stone bladed knife. The innards strained against the hole and bulged out onto the snow as the opening became big enough for them to excape. The warmth of the smooth wet organs was welcome against Broken Jaw's hands. He tugged at the offal, cutting it free at the windpipe and drawing it out while slicing membranes loose from around the lungs. Finally he cut the intestine off as deep within the horse as he could reach. Breathing in the wet odor that rose from the stomach, he pushed the steaming pile away from the horse's open belly. Deftly he cut off one of the front legs at the knee joint, and lay down, pushing his back into the body cavity as far as he could. He shoved the severed leg into the ground in front of him and propped it against the upper part of the rib cage to hold it open. The warmth of the horse's flesh began to penetrate his body and he let himself relax into it.

Deep snow began to pile up, around and over him, creating a mound that blended with the surroundings. Slowly the horse's body began to cool.

Broken Jaw thought about He Walks and Beaver Tail. Surely they had reached the willows by now, and made a shelter by bending over and lashing together young trees. Two men could quickly gather grass and leaves enough to cover such a framework. They even had the deerskin that Beaver Tail always wore about his shoulders. Perhaps they had made a small fire inside their cramped shelter. Broken Jaw shivered and tried not to notice the cold as he thought about the deerskin robe he had left in the lean-to they had constructed the night before. It was certain he would not be returning to that camp until the storm quit.

Strangely, darkness competed with the whiteness and finally won. Broken Jaw shaved slivers of frozen meat from the cut edge of the flanks that sheltered him, and popped the dark red meat into his mouth. With his hands he cleared a breathing space in front of his face. He had a bag filled with dried meat and deer fat tied at his waist, but could not reach his hands around to get it. The horse's ribs were stiff and pressed in on him. His forearms and lower legs stuck out of the cavity he had curled himself into and his fingers and toes sent pain to the center of his stomach. He fought off the feeling of being trapped and let his thinking take him away from the torment.

His thoughts wandered to the camp at the Bent River. The hind leg of elk that hung in camp would last for a few days. If the women could not get to their snares and falling traps, Peeled Hackberry, the shaman, would have to hand out the last of the dried mammoth meat. Broken Jaw felt sleep coming closer as he thought about the small amount of mammoth meat that the shaman had carefully kept from the kill, two seasons before. Like horses, mammoths were rarely seen anymore. He edged closer to sleep, wondering why.

Is Tall had gradually sensed her gracefulness slip away until now she really felt ungainly. Every time she sat cross-legged at the fire, she wondered if she would be able to get up. At these times she would think about turtles. When she was a child, she and her friends delighted in tormenting turtles. They would surround the hapless creature and tease it with a stick. Usually the armored turtle would bite at the branch and hiss its anger at them. Laughing at the creature's discomfort one of the children would flip it onto its back where, unceremoniously, the turtle would struggle to right itself to the amusement of the group circled around it. Inevitably an old woman from camp would break into their fun, and brandishing her fire-hardened digging stick she would steal their turtle. Later, after removing the bottom plate of the turtle's armor and placing hot rocks inside the cavity, the old woman would call the children to a feast of roasted reptile. Now Is Tall understood how the overturned turtle felt and its helplessness became her own.

Her son, Stone Bowl, was approaching his sixth thawing season. Is Tall had been glad to be pregnant again. As Stone Bowl grew older and no baby had taken root inside her, Is Tall had worried that none would. She had been pleased when her moon flow stopped and mornings had caused her stomach to reject food. But now this child inside her was becoming too much to bear. It kicked her ribs so viciously that she almost expected bruises to appear. Other times it seemed to be trying to pry its way out with long fingers.

This was unsettling, making her feel a warmth that Broken Jaw made her feel when he lay close to her at night. She was quite ready to expel this child. Its presence held her in a grip of weariness.

She lay awake waiting for morning to come. Her mate's mother snored loudly in the back of the shelter. Stone Bowl turned over, uncovering himself. In the faint morning light Is Tall reached over and covered her son. The tenderness she felt for him was mixed with the sadness she knew the warm season would bring.

He would be too old to spend his time with her then. He had been a quick learner and now he knew all she had to teach him. With the warm weather would come the beginning of his life as a man. She would not have his company as she gathered wood, set snares and worked hides. They would never again sit together on a hillside and watch ducklings riding on their mother's back in the pond below and laugh when one slid off into the water with a sputter. The secret jokes they shared would no longer be funny. He would even be expected to turn his eyes from her when they met. He would still sleep in her shelter and bring her game from his traps. But they would ignore each other. The seasons they had shared went by too quickly, and now that part of her life and his was almost over.

As she rolled to her side and stiffly got up she thought about the child she would soon have. It was no consolation to her, she missed Stone Bowl already.

The shelter was suffocating her, and she found it hard to breathe. The infant pressed on her lungs from below and a heaviness in her chest pressed from above.

Is Tall hurriedly walked away from camp as far as she could before she had to squat. As she rose her legs were washed with a new flood.

"This child has poked a hole in its bed, it will finally find its way out." She spoke out loud. Her voice startled a crow above her, causing it to scold loudly as it flew off.

She remembered when the water that Stone Bowl had grown in leaked out. She had been excited then. She had welcomed each contraction as they came harder and harder. When she had bitten her lip to keep from crying out, she felt a pride that connected her with all women who had ever embarked upon motherhood. With Stone Bowl it had been different.

She slowly made her way back to her fire and stirred it up. She stared at the extra wood her mate's mother had piled up for the day they would be unable to gather more. That day was here and Is Tall felt no joy. She turned around and saw Broken Jaw's mother watching her. She tried to straighten her shoulders. Without a word between them the older woman took Stone Bowl gently by the hand and led him to the men's fire.

When mid-day came and clouds obscured the sun, Is Tall still sat outside staring into the flames ... waiting.

The wind and the snow came together suddenly. Large flakes swirled around the fire as the mother of Is Tall's mate hurriedly wrapped a few glowing coals with tinder and pushed the fire bundle into a bison horn.

Is Tall tried to get up but a deep pain held her down. The older woman pushed the fire in on itself and covered it with ashes. Despite the cold wind, Is Tall's forehead was wet with sweat. Her fingers clutched the dirt at her side. When the spasm passed, Broken Jaw's mother touched her shoulder lightly.

"Come inside now."

Is Tall could barely hear her over the sound of the wind. Cold flakes of snow melted on her hot forehead. She followed the old woman and bent to enter the shelter, feeling as if her stomach would empty itself through her mouth.

"Your son's mate is trying to make her heart glad, but can not."

She started to smile but the smile crumbled as a tear rolled down her face. Stiffly she turned and lowered the skin flap of the entrance cover.

The old woman nodded as she held a piece of smoking bark next to the grass wick of a stone lamp and blew softly on it. The grease-soaked wick caught the flame and soon the fat surrounding it started to sputter with the heat. It gave off a warm yellow glow that lit up the darkness of the shelter.

The mother of Is Tall's mate sat back on her heels and motioned with her chin toward the sleeping place. Is Tall crawled on her hands and knees to the bison robe and sank down on it.

"When Broken Jaw grew in me I felt like you do now. I was unable to keep food in me. I grew thin while he grew fat!" She held her hands out in front of her as if holding a large belly. "Constantly, I felt as if I had to wet the ground. I wanted it to end, but I did not want him." She shut her eyes and smiled to herself. "My first born slipped out so small that it did not breathe ... even once." Her smile faded. She could barely be heard over the storm. "Perhaps that is why I felt sick ... Now I think I feared that my second child would not live either."

Is Tall looked up at the cratered face that looked soft in the light of the lamp. It was as if she saw her for the first time. She reached for the wrinkled hand and grasped it tightly as another wave of pain flowed over her and crashed against her spine.

The storm's anger raged as the two women struggled. It grew steadily colder outside but the women inside barely noticed. Their breath rose to the poles overhead and froze there. The skin cover at the entrance flapped wildly until the drifting snow packed it in place and silenced it. The fat in the stone lamp melted and the wick threatened to slide into the liquid and drown. Its sputtering distracted the old woman and she lit another lamp before blowing the melted one out. Greasy smoke from the extinguished wick bit into Is Tall's nostrils, but she gave it little notice.

Is Tall's body took over her thoughts so that even Stone Bowl seemed far away and unimportant. Every bit of strength that she had went toward the birthing. There was only the pain and the face of the old woman and the dark walls of the shelter, nothing more. She wasn't even sure that she still existed. It was as though all that was left of her was the middle of her body, which convulsed and ebbed only to gain new strength while she became weaker. The old woman murmured softly to her, but Is Tall was beyond hearing her. The only sound she could hear was the groan that rumbled within her as her body's mightiest effort pushed the child from her. The force that expelled the baby brought a sudden rush of blood that filled the shelter with a hot red smell.

Night was almost gone when Broken Jaw's mother lifted the infant from between Is Tall's legs. He screamed at the cold air that touched his wet skin, and his eyes were clinched tight with his anger. With a piece of ragged deerskin, the old woman dipped into the softened fat of the stone lamp and rubbed grease on the baby's belly. The stump of the blood cord hung from his navel, already shrinking where the old woman had cut it.

Is Tall was breathless and yet felt somehow strengthened from her efforts. The wind still blew as strongly as before, and now she thought of Stone Bowl. Which one of the other shelters had taken him in? Had he heard the cries of his brother.

The old woman laid the naked child next to Is Tall and they both bent over him, touching his body tenderly. He swung his arms and legs furiously. Filling his lungs again and again with air that he turned into howls, he thrashed about as if to turn himself over.

"I'm no longer the turtle ... he is." Is Tall said with quiet surprise.

The two women laughed loudly at the baby until the sound of their laughter caught his attention and he was quiet. With eyes that could not yet focus he stared up at them and made loud sucking noises as part of his fist brushed against his mouth.

"Broken Jaw!"

He heard someone call his name but the voice seemed so far away. His mind was wrapped in a thick fog. What was it he had been dreaming about? Oh ... yes ... the wrestling contest. He was called by the name of Yellow Leaf then, had just passed his eighteenth thawing season, and was thick with muscle and confidence.

The Red Hills People and the High Plains People had gathered to hunt bison, but to a young man the wrestling contests were as important a reason to gather as was the hunt. He and the boy he wrestled were well matched. Neither had been beaten. They both dripped with sweat, and the bright sun glistened on their skin, bare except for the scant loin coverings that were their only garments. Yellow Leaf's eyes were intently locked on his opponent's. They circled with their arms partly flexed and hands open. Broken Jaw made a slight feint to the right and moved in to the left. It worked. Caught slightly off guard, the other boy lost his balance as he was pushed back. But recovery was quick and the advantage was lost as fast as it had been gained. Yellow Leaf soon felt his left arm being pinned back and a knee in the small of his back caused him to buckle. As he went down, he put out his right arm to catch his fall and the lower part of his face crashed into his own hand. He heard a strange crunching sound and felt a tingling in his jaw that quickly turned into a hot pain. He held his jaw in both hands and looked up from his sprawled position to see a tall, thin girl smiling at him. He was never called Yellow Leaf again.

"Broken Jaw!"

There was that voice again, so far away. The dream ... yes ... the tall girl standing there looking at him. She did not seem to pity him, in fact she seemed quite amused. He looked up at her just as she turned and disappeared into the crowd.

"Broken Jaw!"

Why was Beaver Tail's voice in his dream? He

hadn't been there. He had been with the hunters, scouting.

"Broken Jaw!"

The voice was sharp and tried to cut through the warm dream, letting in the cold. Broken Jaw struggled to keep the warmth of the dream, but the silence left behind when the wind stopped blowing struggled to wake him. He could not think. He tried to feel his jaw, but his fingers didn't work. He tried to call out, but his chin was stiff and would not let his mouth make words. His chin had been stiff after he broke his jaw but it had been warm then ... he worked to open his eyes and watched Beaver Tail's face start to shimmer as it turned into a horse dancing on a cloud.

X-tra Pages

*T*he printer says we got to have these extra pages for to fill the book ... so. We got a coupla fire making things that we had decided to leave out because it's for the most part not real practical day to day usage stuff - for all of our real practical day to day primitive living. We'll let the photos do most of the talking.

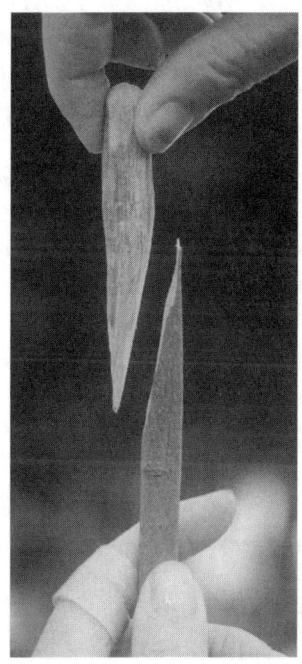

Similar to the splicing done in chapter seven. One just don't always find good hand drills - being able to splice a tip on an otherwise unusable fire drill, hand or bow, can be useful. This is easily accomplished with stone tools.

Fire plow

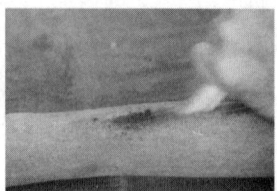

This method of fire making comes to us from the south seas and is as close to just plain rubbing sticks as it gets. The key word is soft - as in soft woods. We here use a yucca flower stalk as the rub-er and a piece of root for the rub-ee. You need dead and soft, not crumbly. Grains of wood play a part here - we get more by running the groove at <u>an off angle to straight</u> on the hearth - at least <u>we</u> feel it gives us more friction.

More dust is made quicker by keeping the flattest part of the yucca in contact and more heat gained by using the point. Begin with easy, controlled strokes to make the groove and dust - end with real fast, short strokes, concentrating the pressure at the tip. It ain't easy! Best to go in tandem keeping the tip in constant contact at the dust when changing. This method is fun and challenging but not practical in a survival situation due to the effort involved and high percentage of failure.

Fire saw

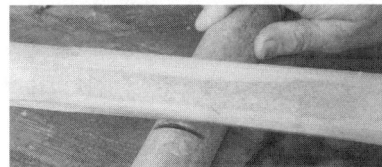

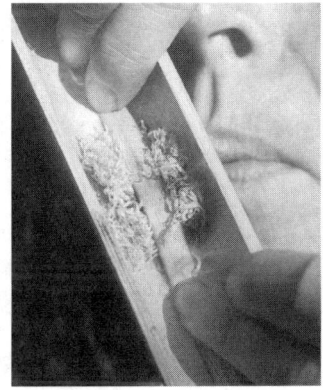

*The fire saw is from the tropics and was first shown here-a-
'bouts by Mtn. Mel DeWeese. Mel spent 20 years teaching
survival to the Navy's finest and picked this up in the Philipines.
The edge of the saw needs to be pretty sharp. The shavings used
here as tinder come from the bamboo itself - this being placed
on either side of the hole from where the dust and coal will fall,
and held in place by a sliver of the bamboo - don't crowd it,
there needs to be space for the dust - and oxygen. One can saw
either downward or with the base up, whichever is more comfortable. Weak pieces will fall apart as considerable stress is
placed on them. This isn't really hard to do - just no bamboo
around most of the USA. With experimentation this could be
applied with other woods.
(Mel is available for modern international survival
instruction at; 1825 Linden, Grand Junction, CO 81503.)*

VIDEOS

As with our book, we began doing videos on these skills because we found that there was not much available for you to choose from that actually worked to **teach you "how-to".** We are especially proud of the two bow videos and feel confident that these are *the* videos to have for both the beginning and advanced bowyer.

Tapes # 1,2,3,6, 9a & 10 are taken from chapters in our book.

#1 Brain Tan Buckskin
Step by step from fresh skin to finished buckskin in as little as 8 hours. Quickest/ easiest way to accomplish this.Our most popular tape. 80 minutes.
$29.95 postpaid

#2 Primitive Fire & Cordage
Three methods of friction fire and cordage from natural materials. Make your own fire by "rubbing sticks" in no time. 100 minutes.
$29.95 postpaid

#3 Primitive Bow & Arrow
From tree to finished bow - & arrow. All steps covered - most importantly the physics explain *why & how* a stick bends. 115 minutes.
$29.95 postpaid

#6 Deer from field to Freezer
Using only common kitchen knives, the McPhersons take a deer sized animal (a goat) from moment of kill to ready to package. 65 minutes.**$29.95** ppd

#9-a - Breaking Rock -
FLINTKNAPPING - Predictably removing flakes from stone - an in depth study of basic percussion flaking - flake by flake unravel the secrets 118 minutes -
$29.95 postpaid

#10 Primitive Shelters
Several building techniques used to construct four different **livable semi-permanent** shelters using common litter and grasses. 90 minutes.
$29.95 postpaid

The ASIATIC COMPOSITE BOW tape is the only complete "how-to" available in any media on this subject that we are aware of.

#GK   How to Construct the Asiatic Composite Bow
This is the **horn and sinew** bow that shot an arrow over half a mile - two hundred years ago. 119 minutes. Jeffrey Schmidt & John McPherson
$39.95 postpaid

Special - 20% discount on all orders over $100.

"Naked into the Wilderness"

Yes!
Please rush me the items noted below!

Name _____

Address _____

City _____ State or Prov. _____ Zip _____

Item	Quantity	Price	Amount
Book NW-1 - "Primitive Wilderness Living & Survival Skills"		x $24.95 =	
Book NW-2 - "Primitive Wilderness Skills, Applied & Advanced"		x $24.95 =	
Videos (please mark appropriate boxes) ☐ #GK Asiatic Composite Bow (@ $39.95)		x $39.95 =	
The below five videos come with the book (chapter) of same title.			
☐ #1 Brain Tan Buckskin (@ $29.95) ☐ #2 Primitive Fire & Cordage (@ $29.95)		x $29.95 =	
☐ #3 Primitive Bow & Arrow (@ $29.95) ☐ #6 Field to Freezer (@ $29.95)		Subtotal	
☐ #9-a Breaking Rock (@ $29.95)		Minus -	
☐ #10 Shelters (@ $29.95)			
		Amount from ABOVE	
		Total $	

- Deduct $5.00 each - when ordering 2 or more large books and/or videos
- **PLUS** - deduct an additional 20% on all orders over $100.00

Postage and All applicable sales taxes included

Order from: **Prairie Wolf**
POB 96
Randolph, KS 66554
www.prairiewolf.net

or - call 1 (800) 258-1232 - or - www.prairiewolf.net